2Corinthians

I0098958

GARY R. SMALL

2 Corinthians
Copyright © 2025 by Gary R. Small

Print ISBN: 978-1-4866-2694-6
eBook ISBN: 978-1-4866-2695-3

Word Alive Press
119 De Baets Street, Winnipeg, MB R2J 3R9
www.wordalivepress.ca

WORD ALIVE
—P R E S S—

Cataloguing in Publication may be obtained through Library and Archives Canada.

Contents

Series Introduction

Keep this Book of the Law always on your lips; meditate on it day and night, so that you may be careful to do everything written in it. Then you will be prosperous and successful. (Joshua 1:8)

The word meditate and its derivatives occur eighteen times in the Bible. Of these, eight pertain to meditating on the Scriptures. Through these verses, we are encouraged to hold God's word in our hearts so that we might profit from His wisdom and be blessed by a closer relationship with Him (Psalm 119:1–3).

The secular world has also proposed the concept of taking a thoughtful approach to life and uses the word mindfulness to describe a thoughtful, meditative approach to life.

Mindfulness has been defined as "the awareness that arises through paying attention in the present moment, on purpose, nonjudgmentally."[1] Other terms have been applied to this intentional approach, such as *to internalize, to meditate on,* or *to process*. It is what we as Christians do when we carefully consider the Bible.

[1] Judson Brewer, *Unwinding Anxiety* (New York, NY: Avery, 2021), 71. Quoting Jon Kabat-Zinn.

The trouble is that we often don't have time to study in this manner. Instead we find ourselves snatching moments in our busy lives to read, internalize, and digest passages from our daily reading of the Bible. By squeezing these most important moments of the day into the least number of minutes, we don't make time for the mindfulness required to truly digest God's word.

Another mistake we often fall into is having too high expectations of ourselves. We lean into weighty commentaries or topical novels on life-changing subjects and once again find that we don't have the sufficient time or headspace to do justice to the meaty subjects therein.

We previously referred to this problem as having too much pace and not sufficient peace to make sense of God's word. It is the challenge that led to the production of this series of books, which are designed to help lift a word from His word and make it poignant.

How we choose to use the selected word for each chapter will be different for each reader. Each chapter is designed to provoke mindful thought on a biblical passage. We have also provided three applications at the end of each chapter to stimulate further reflection.

It is hoped that the chosen word from each passage will be recalled throughout the day when we find moments of stillness or thought, so we can pay attention, on purpose, nonjudgmentally.

These books can be used by individuals. They may also find use in group settings to provoke further discussion on a sermon series or in small group Bible study.

It is hoped that the books will be used as a spiritual tool to reinvigorate your Bible reading and provide impetus to make a life change as a Christian.

The concept is simple, one which by no means seeks to detract from the value of in-depth Bible study. There is still a place for this when time allows and further reading references are provided. We have taken care to tread a middle road theologically and avoid weighty arguments on some finer points of hermeneutics, although some of these can be found within the referenced material.

We sincerely hope that *A Word from His Word* will not only lift selected words from the pages of Scripture but also provide a lift to your Bible reading and spiritual life.

Much has been made by the secular world of the benefits of mindfulness. I suspect this discipline is not new, although it has perhaps been lost in our striving for scientific purpose. Yet there is, in this series, an opportunity to rediscover the usefulness of intentional meditation on God's word (Psalm 1:1–2).

Foreword

One of the gifts of pastoring and being part of a church family is getting to see the quiet faithfulness of people up close—their character, their love for God, and the way they live out what they believe in all areas of life. Gary is one of these gifts and I am very grateful to God for him. His passion for the scriptures, his thoughtful reflections, and his desire to help others grow in faith are very much alive on the pages of this devotional on 2 Corinthians.

This book isn't just theological—it's pastoral. Gary doesn't try to impress you with deep or lofty arguments (though he could). Instead he gently invites you to pause, reflect, and consider a single word or truth from each passage. He helps us sit with truth—not rushing past it, not overcomplicating it, but letting it shape our hearts one word at a time. Each reflection creates space for meditation, application, and transformation. It's the kind of devotional that meets you where you are but doesn't leave you there; it helps you go deeper in your faith and encourages a greater desire for following after Jesus.

2 Corinthians is a letter that pulls no punches. It's full of raw honesty, hope, hardship, and grace. And in these pages, Gary

walks with us through it—not as a lecturer, but as a fellow learner and follower of Jesus.

Whether you're reading this with your morning coffee, in a small group, or on your lunch break, I pray that you experience the same thing Gary clearly has: the Word of God coming alive, speaking clearly, and calling us closer to Jesus. I pray that, like Paul's hope for the Corinthians, your heart would be made "wide open" through what you read in A Word from His Word—softened, strengthened, and stirred to respond to the Holy Spirit.

Thank you, Gary, for sharing your heart in this profound yet practical study of 2 Corinthians with us. It's a gift.

—Caleb Groeneweg
Lead Pastor, LOCAL Church
Ottawa, Ontario

Introduction

When we open our Bibles, we hope for inspiration. We go to be lifted from our grey moods, be carried when we feel tired. These moments are like the dawn of a new day. We feel hope and know there will be opportunities, but we also recognize that there will be challenges.

Just as we feel nervous in the early morning concerning the day ahead, we feel a degree of nervous anticipation about embarking on a read of 2 Corinthians. This letter comes with a reputation.

It is not a light read. We might approach it like we would a respected boxing opponent or a mountain climb of renowned difficulty. Just like those formidable challenges, mastering 2 Corinthians promises to leave us with lasting lessons.

In 2 Corinthians, Paul seeks to deeply impress on us an imprint of Christ. Its familiar challenge is to attempt this in a population resistant to elevating God above secular or practical philosophy. To further add to the challenge, Paul was attempting this while having his own credentials discredited.

Dating 2 Corinthians requires us to rely on some of the information Paul gave regarding different travel plans throughout the letter. If 1 Corinthians was written in AD 53 or 54, to allow for favourable travelling seasons for Timothy, Paul, and Titus, the composition of 2 Corinthians would have taken place in AD 55 or 56.

Paul indicates that he wrote from Macedonia, or northern Greece. This would have occurred on his third missionary journey, which places us in the same timeframe as Acts 20. In Acts, Luke doesn't say whether Paul stayed in Thessalonica, Berea, or even Philippi to write. Paul himself doesn't reveal his location either. It is apparent that he was a free man, just as he was when he wrote 1 Corinthians, and in all probability he was travelling from city to city in Macedonia, composing the letter while on the move.

It is also noteworthy that Luke makes no mention in Acts about the disunity brewing in Corinth.

Another obstacle which prevents an accurate dating of 2 Corinthians is the possibility that the letter consists of more than one piece of correspondence. In addition, there may be lost letters to the Corinthians. It appears that Paul wrote four letters to the church in Corinth. Ben Witherington labels them Corinthians A, B, C, and D. Corinthians A is referred to as an earlier correspondence, mentioned in 1 Corinthians 5:9. The text of 1 Corinthians constitutes Corinthians B. Corinthians C is often referred to as the *painful letter* mentioned in 2 Corinthians 7:8. Finally, Corinthians D is the text we know of as 2 Corinthians.[2]

Some scholars argue that 2 Corinthians 1–9 and 2 Corinthians 10–13 represent two different correspondences, with the

---

[2] Ben Witherington III, *Conflict and Community in Corinth: A Sociorhetorical Commentary on 1 and 2 Corinthians* (Grand Rapids, MI: Eerdmans, 1995), 329–330.

latter being the *painful letter*. Others argue that 2 Corinthians should be considered a single communication. This is how we will approach it.

If 1 Corinthians was a letter intended to bring some in the Corinthian church back into line with the gospel, then 2 Corinthians attempts to reconcile the Corinthians with Paul. Such was the degree of rebellion; some had determined Paul to be in error and had decided to discredit his status as an apostle and ambassador of Christ.

In writing, Paul sought to rebut those who would dismiss his credentials and re-sow foundational gospel truths into the Corinthian church. He sought reconciliation with those who would be not reconciled. He tried to reason with those who thought they knew better than him, and with those who had been convinced of their superior understanding through the teaching of false apostles.

There were several culture clashes between Paul and some in the Corinthian church. Paul's leadership style of humble deference to God and Jesus was at odds with the perspectives of some in first-century Corinth.

In Corinth, those who had a tangible public presence tended to be held in high esteem. The Corinthians applauded those who were able to hold their own in public debates, who were grandiose and formidable in their arguments. In classical Greek style, they looked for leaders who would have been at home in the 14,000-seat theatre found in Corinth.

Although Paul was seemingly at home debating in the synagogue, he was forever reluctant to pursue complex arguments, at least in public, choosing to present the cross and allow God's revelation to ignite the hearts of his listeners.

He was also reluctant to receive patronage for his speeches, which seemed at odds with the natural order of philosophers at that time. It was more usual for spiritual or philosophical leaders to be under the patronage of a wealthy individual. Both benefitted from the arrangement, the patron from having their popularity enhanced by their association with a famous figure, and the speaker from being given a lifestyle beyond their means. Paul rejected such speaker privileges, opting to earn his living from tentmaking and recommending any would-be benefactors to support the church in Jerusalem though an offering he organized.

As well as these personal attacks on Paul's persona, other causes of conflict were of a theological nature. These took the familiar pattern of attacks from Jewish Christians emphasizing the salvific nature of the law, opining on the importance of abiding by food restrictions and Sabbath practices.

True to the form he expressed in his other letters, Paul would not stand for any dilution of the gospel by suggesting such practices could add to the saving grace of Christ. It is not surprising then that there would be some conflict in these areas, as a post-Jesus understanding of holiness was worked out.

This letter has challenges and we will encounter some tough lessons. We should note at the outset, though, that Paul, despite the possible opposition he could have experienced, did return to Corinth. His return was not characterized by riots or demonstrations as far as history records. Nor was he arrested. It is to be hoped that peace and unity were restored to the church during his return.

At his return, he also collected the offering for the Jerusalem church. The presence of the offering itself intimates the willingness of some to change from their prior traditions and adopt Pauline practices.

I also find it provocative that toward the end of Paul's life, in his letters to Titus and Timothy, he chose Ephesus for Timothy and Crete for Titus. Neither were sent back for another mission in Corinth. Perhaps lessons were learned by those in Achaia who heard Paul's wisdom in 2 Corinthians and unity with the gospel was restored.

Our wrestles with God are not so different from those of the Corinthians. We have an expectation of strong, influential leaders. We hope for charismatic, eloquent preachers who will have an answer for all the world's problems, especially those closest to our hearts. We too hope that our preachers might share some of our deepest grievances and fight for them on our behalf, especially if we support them.

Given this commonality with the Corinthians, we are going to find ourselves reminded by Paul that our focus should always be on Christ.

We might have superficial desires which can be easily swayed by the world's perspectives. But there are deeper truths—truths which, should we choose to follow them, will bring us closer to God and enable the ending of our moments with His word to be just as optimistic as the beginning.

A NOTE ON PAUL'S APOSTOLIC AUTHORITY

Clearly, then, to read 2 Corinthians without reflecting on the assumptions of authority with which Paul wrote would be to miss one of the essential points of the text. In studying this letter, we are studying God's Word, and in studying God's Word we are obligated to submit to its truth and relevancy for our lives. Paul's apostolic authority was not the product of his own initiative, cleverness, people skills, political savvy, or education. In 2 Corinthians Paul is not the CEO of a corporation fighting to keep his career or a personnel manager struggling with administering his human resources. Although 2 Corinthians contains a powerful polemic on behalf of Paul's ministry, the urgency of his self defense derives from the fact that, as "an apostle of Christ Jesus," he represents Christ himself rather than his own personal interests.[3]

---

[3] Scott J. Hafemann, *2 Corinthians: The NIV Application Commentary* (Grand Rapids, MI: Zondervan, 2000), 56.

Church

2 CORINTHIANS 1:1–2

Paul, an apostle of Christ Jesus by the will of God, and Timothy our brother, to the church of God in Corinth, together with all his holy people throughout Achaia: ² Grace and peace to you from God our Father and the Lord Jesus Christ.

We all have items and relationships that are precious to us. They hold worth and are meaningful to us. If we were to lose them, we would be emotionally hurt. Family, marriage partners, and children are good examples of worthwhile relationships. Material items would include houses, heirlooms, precious photographs, and tokens of love such as wedding rings. Some might list possessions like restored vintages cars, cherished bicycles, or favourite sweaters.

For Paul, his most precious possession wasn't a vintage car or even his tentmaking kit; it was his faith. This was followed closely by his relationship with the church. His association with fellow believers was highly cherished.

In the same way, our relationships with people are precious. We don't own or control them. In this, there is a subtle but important distinction worth pointing out.

At the beginning of 2 Corinthians, Paul wasn't seeking to control or own the church but to restore his relationship with them and for them to restore their relationship with God.

The Greek word *ekklesia*, used by Paul in 2 Corinthians 1:1 for church, describes the gathering of Christians in fellowship.

Ekklesia is a compound word formed from *ek*, meaning "out of," and *kaleo*, meaning "to call." It was used by the Greeks to describe the assembly of responsible people called out from the population to help make important community decisions. Today, we might opt for the word council.

Previously, the people of Israel had represented God on the earth. They were the chosen people, the called-out ones, the *ekklesia*. In the Greek translation of the Old Testament, the Hebrew word for assembly was translated as *ekklesia*.

Paul appreciated that a shift had occurred with the birth of Christ. *Ekklesia* no longer just referred to the Jews; it now included Jews and Gentiles. Through Christ, salvation came to anyone who would believe in Jesus.

In using this term, Paul reflected not just the formation of a new religious organization (the Christian church) but also passed comment on the Corinthians. They were now called-out ones, included as Gentiles and Hellenistic Jews into the saving grace of God.

Unity within the new *ekklesia* was important to Paul, for Christ had paid for this unity and it had come at great cost. In order for this precious unity to rule, Paul understood that the *ekklesia* would have to follow the gospel. This entailed listening to apostles who had been directly sent from Christ with the gospel.

Church: 2 Corinthians 1:1-2

In his standard opening lines to this letter, Paul sets himself up to defend the *ekklesia* and his relationship with it. We note his insistence on mentioning his qualifications as an apostle, as well as his support for his co-defendant Timothy and how he saw the assembly in Corinth. He saw them as a justifiable council to represent God on the earth. They were the called-out ones, holy and set apart to do God's work.

He confirmed the sincerity of his opening address with a personal greeting from the one who had sent him: the Lord Jesus.

We don't reflect enough on the preciousness of the church in our lives. Sadly, we tend to spend more time considering other elements, both material and relational. Paul's opening verses give us pause to think on the concept of church as those who have been called out by Christ to do His work and be His representatives. This is a heady responsibility, but one in which He supports us and one He hopes is precious to us.

APPLICATION: CHURCH

- I suspect that not many would put church at the top of the list of what they find precious. Pray for God to change our perspective on the church and for us to perceive its value afresh.
- Next time you attend church, consider those around you have also been called out as being precious to God and dignified by His Son. Thank God for their presence in your church.

- Think of ways in which you can express the value you attribute to your church. This might be done practically with an act of service or through a simple commitment to pray for its continued witness.

Trust

Praise be to the God and Father of our Lord Jesus Christ, the Father of compassion and the God of all comfort, [4] who comforts us in all our troubles, so that we can comfort those in any trouble with the comfort we ourselves receive from God. [5] For just as we share abundantly in the sufferings of Christ, so also our comfort abounds through Christ. [6] If we are distressed, it is for your comfort and salvation; if we are comforted, it is for your comfort, which produces in you patient endurance of the same sufferings we suffer. [7] And our hope for you is firm, because we know that just as you share in our sufferings, so also you share in our comfort.

[8] We do not want you to be uninformed, brothers and sisters, about the troubles we experienced in the province of Asia. We were under great pressure, far beyond our ability to endure, so that we despaired of life itself. [9] Indeed, we felt we had received the sentence of death. But this happened that we might not rely on ourselves but on God, who raises the dead. [10] He has delivered us from such a deadly peril, and he will deliver us again. On him we have set our hope that he will

continue to deliver us, [11] as you help us by your prayers. Then many will give thanks on our behalf for the gracious favor granted us in answer to the prayers of many.

Paul's opening paragraphs of 2 Corinthians are unorthodox. If you were to write a reconciliatory letter, having earlier penned a painful one, I suspect you wouldn't begin by discussing suffering. To begin so could serve as a reminder of what was said previously and open old wounds.

I think it would have been safer to have opened with a more positive welcome. Instead we have a beginning that catches us off-guard.

It makes me question what news of Corinth Titus passed on. In order for Paul to start with suffering, had Titus suggested that the Corinthians found Paul too uncaring or unresponsive to their own hardships?

Perhaps, as in 1 Corinthians when Paul starts with the cross to establish one's dependency on God, in 2 Corinthians he wishes to point directly to God from the start. He seeks to anchor everything that follows to a reliance on God.

Rather than discussing Christ's suffering on the cross, which was the strategy in 1 Corinthians, Paul chooses here to discuss his and Timothy's own tribulations. He comes to this point in 2 Corinthians 1:9, stating that at their lowest point they were forced to rely on God rather than their own means. The word rely is translated from the Greek *pepoithotes*, which means trusting or having confidence in something. At their weakest, when distress was set to overwhelm them, Paul and Timothy found the will to go on by trusting in God.

It seems likely that Paul hoped the Corinthians too would trust God in their difficulties. Perhaps it was his aim to instill empathy in them and pass on his own blueprint of how to work through tough times.

In the face of suffering, Paul doesn't make the case for lamenting to God for the difficulties he experienced, although there are precedents for this in Psalms and Lamentations. Nor does Paul come close to a James-like emphasis: *"Consider it pure joy… whenever you face trials of many kinds… "* (James 1:2) Rather, when hardships occur, he recommends that we embrace our trust in God.

Paul had an unshakable belief in the sovereignty of God and wished the Corinthians would see this and make it their own. For Paul, whether life was easy or hard, there was always God. God doesn't change. His constancy or sovereignty keeps our world in balance. He will be there in the morning and in the evening, no matter what might befall us during the day. His presence is constant.

Just like the petrol needed to run a car, God runs our world. So if a car breaks down, it will still need petrol to start moving again, whether an engine part is replaced, a puncture fixed, or windscreen repaired. The reliance on petrol is constant. We might say that even when the car is in distress, it needs petrol. We might say that petrol has sovereign rule over the car.

For Paul, the constancy of God was like this. It didn't matter whether he was running smoothy or stuttering along; God was steadfast and compassionate. Paul had mirrored God's compassion to the Corinthians. Here he sought to do it again, wanting them to appreciate, despite the setbacks he had experienced in Macedonia, that he and Timothy continued to trust in the compassion of God.

Paul knew it would be important to instill this deep-seated trust in God into the Corinthians if they were to turn an ear to the rest of his letter. Without a trusting foundation in God, it was unlikely they would be interested in travelling further.

APPLICATION: TRUST

- Our petrol analogy is weak, but it demonstrates how fruitless it is to blame God for life's struggles. We wouldn't yell at the petrol pump when we suffer a puncture, or when our starter engine is broken. Nor should we call into question the sovereignty or benevolence of God when life throws us a curve ball.

- Take a moment today to remember and thank God for His forever presence.

- Consider how your vehicle is ruled by its requirement on fuel. It will still require fuel if something breaks, just as we still need God if things aren't going the way we planned. Like Paul, pray that you would know God's comfort, especially when life is hard.

- Trust in a benevolent God when we're suffering isn't easy, but Paul encourages us not to give up. Persistence in our belief will bring us hope, and deliver hope to those around us. Pray that those who are suffering would be given the strength and support to persevere in their witness.

Sincerity

2 CORINTHIANS 1:12–2:11

Now this is our boast: Our conscience testifies that we have conducted ourselves in the world, and especially in our relations with you, with integrity and godly sincerity. We have done so, relying not on worldly wisdom but on God's grace. [13] For we do not write you anything you cannot read or understand. And I hope that, [14] as you have understood us in part, you will come to understand fully that you can boast of us just as we will boast of you in the day of the Lord Jesus.

[15] Because I was confident of this, I wanted to visit you first so that you might benefit twice. [16] I wanted to visit you on my way to Macedonia and to come back to you from Macedonia, and then to have you send me on my way to Judea. [17] Was I fickle when I intended to do this? Or do I make my plans in a worldly manner so that in the same breath I say both "Yes, yes" and "No, no"?

[18] But as surely as God is faithful, our message to you is not "Yes" and "No." [19] For the Son of God, Jesus Christ, who was preached among you by us—by me and Silas and Timothy—was not "Yes" and "No," but in him it has always been "Yes." [20] For no matter how

many promises God has made, they are "Yes" in Christ. And so through him the "Amen" is spoken by us to the glory of God. [21] Now it is God who makes both us and you stand firm in Christ. He anointed us, [22] set his seal of ownership on us, and put his Spirit in our hearts as a deposit, guaranteeing what is to come.

[23] I call God as my witness—and I stake my life on it—that it was in order to spare you that I did not return to Corinth. [24] Not that we lord it over your faith, but we work with you for your joy, because it is by faith you stand firm.

[1] So I made up my mind that I would not make another painful visit to you. [2] For if I grieve you, who is left to make me glad but you whom I have grieved? [3] I wrote as I did, so that when I came I would not be distressed by those who should have made me rejoice. I had confidence in all of you, that you would all share my joy. [4] For I wrote you out of great distress and anguish of heart and with many tears, not to grieve you but to let you know the depth of my love for you.

[5] If anyone has caused grief, he has not so much grieved me as he has grieved all of you to some extent—not to put it too severely. [6] The punishment inflicted on him by the majority is sufficient. [7] Now instead, you ought to forgive and comfort him, so that he will not be overwhelmed by excessive sorrow. [8] I urge you, therefore, to reaffirm your love for him. [9] Another reason I wrote you was to see if you would stand the test and

be obedient in everything. [10] Anyone you forgive, I also forgive. And what I have forgiven—if there was anything to forgive—I have forgiven in the sight of Christ for your sake, [11] in order that Satan might not outwit us. For we are not unaware of his schemes.

We noted in the opening verses that some in the Corinthian church had trust issues. They had begun to distrust God since His messenger had suffered, which seemed unbecoming for an agent of the Most High. To rebuild their trust, Paul pointed to God sovereignty and benevolence.

In our current passage, Paul sought to buttress those ideas by highlighting his sincerity in three areas: communication, travel arrangements, and church discipline.

In 2 Corinthians 1:12, Paul prefaces the remainder of the passage by indicating:

> Now this is our boast: Our conscience testifies that we have conducted ourselves in the world, and especially in our relations with you, with integrity and godly sincerity. We have done so, relying not on worldly wisdom but on God's grace.

The word translated sincerity is from the Greek *eilikrineia*, which is a composite of *heile*, meaning the shining of the sun, and *krino*, meaning to judge. An item that stood the test of being held up to bright sunlight was considered to be genuine and flawless.

Ancient fine pottery was thin and often cracked during fabrication. To seal the cracks, potters would use wax. Once glazed and painted, the wax was indistinguishable from the surrounding pottery and masked any imperfections. To reveal flaws, an astute buyer would hold up the pottery to the sunlight shining through the wax.

Our word sincere comes from the Latin equivalent of *eilikirneia*, which simply means without (*sin*) wax (*cera*).

Paul's aim was to rebuild the trust of some in the Corinthian church who had become disillusioned with the apostle as a result of him not fitting their mould for someone who representing the most high God. By emphasizing his sincerity, Paul hoped they might understand that his decisions came from a pure heart.

The words integrity and godly, which refer to Paul's sincerity in 1 Corinthians 1:12, are written as one word in the original. Scholars have disputed whether this word derives from the Greek term for "holiness" or for "pure motives," contesting that a simple scribing error may have led to either. Pure motives would make this a more familiar Pauline term, but holiness also conveys his message. In fact, either qualifier expresses the godly nature of the sincerity he hopes to impress upon his readers so they understand there were no hidden agendas for his changing plans.

It isn't easy to decipher what transpired with Paul's travel arrangements. It would appear that after his initial visit he returned to visit the Corinthians a second time. This was a painful occasion. It appears he hoped to make a third visit, too, but had failed to do so at the time of the letter's writing. His failure to come back appears to have solidified the views of some who discredited Paul.

However, he says that his absence was due to less obvious but still valid wisdom: he chose not to cause more upset and instead wrote them the lost *painful letter*. (2 Corinthians 2:4).

In 2 Corinthians 2:10–11, Paul underlines what lay beneath the purity of his sincerity. He was aware that every church conflict has a spiritual aspect, and being aware of the devil's schemes enables a church to muster a more robust defence.

We further note in 2 Corinthians 2:10 that Paul examines his motives in the sight of Christ. We might say that he uses "Son light" to examine his imperfections, ensuring that his sincerity is genuine whether it comes through in forgiving others, communication, or itinerary planning.

APPLICATION: SINCERITY

- Without-wax is a thought-provoking metaphor to describe the purity of our characters. It is a challenging standard of Christianity: to be so pure and mindful of God's purposes that our own are relegated. Pray that we would hold up our plans to Son light to test them against His standards.
- We can misjudge other Christians by not understanding the meaning of their decisions. Pray for patience and understanding that we might better understand one another.
- Paul reaffirms the godly nature of his character at the outset of this passage to engender trust from the Cor-

inthians. Pray for those who lead your church, that their sincerity would be pure and your trust in them as God's ministers firmly established.

Letters

Now when I went to Troas to preach the gospel of Christ and found that the Lord had opened a door for me, [13] I still had no peace of mind, because I did not find my brother Titus there. So I said goodbye to them and went on to Macedonia.

[14] But thanks be to God, who always leads us as captives in Christ's triumphal procession and uses us to spread the aroma of the knowledge of him everywhere. [15] For we are to God the pleasing aroma of Christ among those who are being saved and those who are perishing. [16] To the one we are an aroma that brings death; to the other, an aroma that brings life. And who is equal to such a task? [17] Unlike so many, we do not peddle the word of God for profit. On the contrary, in Christ we speak before God with sincerity, as those sent from God.

[1] Are we beginning to commend ourselves again? Or do we need, like some people, letters of recommendation to you or from you? [2] You yourselves are our letter, written on our hearts, known and read by everyone.

[3] You show that you are a letter from Christ, the result of our ministry, written not with ink but with the Spirit of the living God, not on tablets of stone but on tablets of human hearts.

In these verses, Paul draws on the writings of Ezekiel to explain what he perceives has occurred with the Corinthians:

I will give them an undivided heart and put a new spirit in them; I will remove from them their heart of stone and give them a heart of flesh. (Ezekiel 11:19; see similar in Ezekiel 36:26–27)

Paul considered the Corinthians to have changed their hearts from being worldly to being engraved by God. They had given over ownership of their hearts, allowing His name to be engraved on them. They were now driven by God's indelible mark on their soul. No longer did their hearts beat to a self-orchestrated tune; rather, they hummed to the words inscribed upon their surface. Those words came from the Spirit of the living God, which was alive and coursing within their hearts.

It is a vivid image, and that was Paul's aim. He wished to break away from staid, crusty images of religion. Instead he hoped to highlight how being in a relationship with the living God was different from the prior beliefs held by the Corinthians. It was different than holding to the stone tablets of the law, different than believing in an inanimate statue of a Greek or Roman god.

Paul wrote that there was a vibrancy to Christianity, a vibrancy which the Corinthians exhibited. Their portrayal of the Christian life became like a letter written about Jesus. Paul also described the Corinthians as his own letters of recommendation (2 Corinthians 3:2). Their lives said so much more than he could put down on paper; they were a better commendation to his own credibility than a simple written reference.

In other words, he used the changed lives of the Corinthians to argue for His own credibility. Paul saw something of God's claim on his own life in the lives of some of the Corinthians. He recognized that their hearts had been changed.

He shared this imagery with them not to boast of his own achievements but rather to encourage them, just as a teacher does with their pupil or a parent does with their child. The Corinthians themselves were his biggest defence. They spoke to his credibility as an apostle and to the credibility of a loving, living God. They were his letters of recommendation.

APPLICATION: LETTERS

- How do those whom you have discipled or mentored reflect your Christianity? For Paul, the Corinthians were letters of commendation to the purity of his message and the integrity of his life. Take your thoughts to God in prayer.
- The converse is also true: we reflect our teachers and our pastors. Pray that we would represent those who serve us.

- Although it's a play on Paul's idea, we might stretch his metaphor to include letters of professional qualification. What would our letters indicate about our integrity?

Grammar

2 CORINTHIANS 3:4–6

Such confidence we have through Christ before God.
[5] Not that we are competent in ourselves to claim anything for ourselves, but our competence comes from
God. [6] He has made us competent as ministers of a new
covenant—not of the letter but of the Spirit; for the letter kills, but the Spirit gives life.

We miss something of the force of these verses in the New
International Version. In just a few lines, Paul covers
important differences between the Old Testament covenant and
the covenant ushered in by Christ. His forthright approach suggests that he had previously taught the Corinthians about the finer
details, which is why here he is able to keep his larger discussion
confined to his competency and validity as an apostle.

We should note that the change in direction between the
covenants is linked to Paul's credibility. The changes themselves
are manifested in the message Paul preached.

In 2 Corinthians 3:6, Paul declares, *"He has made us competent as ministers of a new covenant—not of the letter but of the Spirit;
for the letter kills, but the Spirit gives life."*

The word ministers comes from the Greek word *diakonous*, which might be better translated as "servant of the king." Paul saw himself as serving Christ's new covenant, a covenant that wasn't based on the law.

If we look again at this verse, we may note that Paul doesn't use the word law. We subconsciously interpret "letter" to mean this. "Letter" here would be better translated as grammar or punctuation, for it is translated from the Greek word *gramma*, not from *epistol*. *Gramma* might be also understood as referring to the letters of the alphabet.

Paul's point was that it was Jewish attitudes to the law that led them away from God rather than the law itself. Their focus on grammar, punctuation, or legalism prevented their spiritual vitality.

In the new covenant, we receive the Holy Spirit rather than more of the law. The Holy Spirit is our stamp of reassurance that we have been given spiritual life.

Just as it was the attitude toward the law that corrupted the purposes of the law, so to our attitude toward the new covenant needs to be kept in check, lest it too becomes corrupted.

It is just as possible to become too "grammarly" about our Christianity, and in our legalese we may miss the essence of spirituality to which we have been called and born into: *"for the letter kills, but the Spirit gives life."*

APPLICATION: GRAMMAR

- Pray that the Holy Spirit would continue to work in your heart to diminish righteousness and promote life.

- When read as referring to grammar, or legalese, instead of "letter," 2 Corinthians 3:6 transforms into a challenge to those in the Corinthian church who were standing in judgment of Paul's life and ministry style. When tempted to be critical of our pastors, we would do well to remember Paul's challenge and rethink our comments.

- Thank Jesus for His gift of the Holy Spirit and spend a moment in quiet reflection that we might hear His voice.

Unveiled

2 CORINTHIANS 3:7–18

Now if the ministry that brought death, which was engraved in letters on stone, came with glory, so that the Israelites could not look steadily at the face of Moses because of its glory, transitory though it was, [8] will not the ministry of the Spirit be even more glorious? [9] If the ministry that brought condemnation was glorious, how much more glorious is the ministry that brings righteousness! [10] For what was glorious has no glory now in comparison with the surpassing glory. [11] And if what was transitory came with glory, how much greater is the glory of that which lasts!

[12] Therefore, since we have such a hope, we are very bold. [13] We are not like Moses, who would put a veil over his face to prevent the Israelites from seeing the end of what was passing away. [14] But their minds were made dull, for to this day the same veil remains when the old covenant is read. It has not been removed, because only in Christ is it taken away. [15] Even to this day when Moses is read, a veil covers their hearts. [16] But whenever anyone turns to the Lord, the veil is taken away. [17] Now the Lord is

the Spirit, and where the Spirit of the Lord is, there is freedom. [18] And we all, who with unveiled faces contemplate the Lord's glory, are being transformed into his image with ever-increasing glory, which comes from the Lord, who is the Spirit.

The word unveiled in 2 Corinthians 3:17 is translated from the Greek word *anakekalymmeno*. *Kalymma* is the Greek term for "veil" and *ana* is translated as "upwards" or "back" and here denotes a reversal of veiling.

In these verses, Paul was asserting something quite profound to the Corinthians.

He had been building an image of the gospel. He didn't have the New Testament accounts to sketch out what Jesus's life was like, so he had been using what he did have: the promises of God through the prophets in the Old Testament.

He had raised the idea of having a new heart (2 Corinthians 3:2)—a heart sensitive to God, receptive to His Spirit, and carrying the characteristic handprint of God. To convey an example of this new heart, Paul had reached into the writings of Ezekiel.

Now he reached again into the Old Testament, this time to draw comparisons between Moses and himself. His motives were both to confirm his apostleship to those who doubted and encourage the Corinthians to understand more of the gift that Christ's coming had delivered.

Both Paul and Moses had begun a ministry (2 Corinthians 3:7–11), Moses carrying stone tablets of the law down from Mount Sinai and Paul bringing the story of Jesus's life from across the Mediterranean. The similarities in their messages, though, seemed to end there.

Moses's message led to condemnation and judgment. It had arrived with glory, carved out by God, decreed by His mighty hand, served up with mystery atop Mount Sinai, and delivered to the people through His most faithful servant—but it was destined to fail. Man on his own was too weak to uphold it.

The law was full of godly wisdom, but it would become a tool of judgment rather than a golden blessing. It would become a standard by which failure was measured, not a threshold beyond which all lived in harmony.

Paul stoked this idea of the holy relic of the law being delivered with fanfare and ceremony, highlighting the gloriousness of the gift from God. He built the imagery of the law as an amazing gift only to compare the stone tablets with the miracle of Jesus's life.

Even without his readers' historical or traditional background, we can readily understand and see the meagreness of the law when compared to the magnificence of Christ.

The difference in glory wasn't just marked by the difference between inanimate blocks of rock and a living, breathing human being. Nor was it about differences in the currency of the messages, for God loved the Israelites and He continued to love the Jews.

What distinguished the messages was their scale. Jesus was an order of magnitude greater than the tablets of stone. God's love, expressed through His Son, outshone, outclassed, and superseded all previous expressions, including the stone tablets of the law, great as they were.

Paul drew out his comparison with Moses and the law to highlight the folly of those who hadn't fully grasped the magnitude of the gospel. He referred to the new ministry as the ministry of the Spirit, reflecting the gift Jesus had secured. He contrasted the temporary nature of the law to the lasting ministry of the Spirit, which not only lasts but confirms our right standing with the Father.

Moses used a veil to hide God's glory so as to protect the Israelites from feeling condemned (Exodus 34:33–35). Paul used the notion of a veil to communicate a lack of perception. Only through perceiving who Christ was could the veil be removed.

Paul had experienced such an unveiling on the road to Damascus. In his unveiled state, Paul was converted to Christianity and turned to the Lord. He accepted the Lord's Spirit, and in doing so he now radiated the Lord's glory like a mirror.[4] Furthermore, his radiance of God's glory increased as he grew in Christian maturity (2 Corinthians 3:18).

Conversion to Christianity is so much more than simply conceding the truth of a historical Jesus. Paul believed that conversion affected the heart, the spirit, and perhaps even the complexion. The new spiritual understanding, or second birth, brought a change to a person's demeanour and bearing to reflect God's glory (2 Corinthians 3:18).

---

[4] The word "contemplated" in 2 Corinthians 3:18 is translated from the Greek word *katoptrizomenoi*, meaning "to behold as in a mirror."

APPLICATION: UNVEILED

- In today's verses, Paul grew the idea of an unveiling being synonymous with conversion. Take a moment to consider the impact of your conversion. How do you now see the world differently?
- We have been unveiled through Christ (2 Corinthians 3:14). Pray for your faith to come into the glow of God's presence and rely on Jesus to remain unveiled and not condemned.
- Is it possible that remnants of veiled thinking persist in your spiritual outlook? Ask God to help you unveil any such areas.

This is how the gospel is defined. When we are converted through faith in Christ, what we see with the eyes of our hearts is "the light of the gospel of the glory of Christ, who is the image of God" (2 Corinthians 4:4). The gospel is the good news of all conquering beauty. Or to say it the way Paul does, it is the good news of "the glory of Christ." When we embrace Christ, we embrace God. We see and savor God's glory. There is no savoring of God's glory if we do not see it in Christ. This is the only window through which a sinner may see the face of God and not be incinerated.[5]

---

[5] John Piper, *Don't Waste Your Life* (Wheaton, IL: Crossway, 2009), 40.

Jars of Clay

2 CORINTHIANS 4:1–18

Therefore, since through God's mercy we have this ministry, we do not lose heart. [2] Rather, we have renounced secret and shameful ways; we do not use deception, nor do we distort the word of God. On the contrary, by setting forth the truth plainly we commend ourselves to everyone's conscience in the sight of God. [3] And even if our gospel is veiled, it is veiled to those who are perishing. [4] The god of this age has blinded the minds of unbelievers, so that they cannot see the light of the gospel that displays the glory of Christ, who is the image of God. [5] For what we preach is not ourselves, but Jesus Christ as Lord, and ourselves as your servants for Jesus' sake. [6] For God, who said, "Let light shine out of darkness," made his light shine in our hearts to give us the light of the knowledge of God's glory displayed in the face of Christ.

[7] But we have this treasure in jars of clay to show that this all-surpassing power is from God and not from us. [8] We are hard pressed on every side, but not crushed; perplexed, but not in despair; [9] persecuted, but not abandoned; struck down, but not destroyed.

[10] We always carry around in our body the death of Jesus, so that the life of Jesus may also be revealed in our body. [11] For we who are alive are always being given over to death for Jesus' sake, so that his life may also be revealed in our mortal body. [12] So then, death is at work in us, but life is at work in you.

[13] It is written: "I believed; therefore I have spoken." Since we have that same spirit of faith, we also believe and therefore speak, [14] because we know that the one who raised the Lord Jesus from the dead will also raise us with Jesus and present us with you to himself. [15] All this is for your benefit, so that the grace that is reaching more and more people may cause thanksgiving to overflow to the glory of God.

[16] Therefore we do not lose heart. Though outwardly we are wasting away, yet inwardly we are being renewed day by day. [17] For our light and momentary troubles are achieving for us an eternal glory that far outweighs them all. [18] So we fix our eyes not on what is seen, but on what is unseen, since what is seen is temporary, but what is unseen is eternal.

In 2 Corinthians 4, Paul continued to justify his ministry. In doing so, he highlighted what pure ministry should look like. Recall that Paul railed against teachers who came to Corinth after him and convinced some in the Corinthian church of false teachings. These teachers questioned the validity of Paul's apostolic calling, and in response to their accusations Paul set out the simplicity and purity of his message. He didn't rely on persuasive words or try to alter God's message (2 Corinthians 4:2). Rather, he chose to preach only about Jesus.

Paul had already defended his history of persecution and proposed that this was evidence in favour of His commission by God. He now reaffirmed this position and reflected on how responsibility for the gospel had been secured within fragile jars of clay (2 Corinthians 4:7). Paul's point was that such a strategy would require God's intervention to succeed.

The word clay is translated from the Greek *ostrakinos*, which refers to baked clay. Such items were considered the least valuable of household items, incredibly fragile and prone to breakage.

Commentators have suggested that Paul used this comparison for one of two possible reasons, or perhaps both of them.

The first contrasts the mundane nature of the jar with the rich treasure of the gospel. This comparison serves to capture something of the immense blessing of the gospel story, how a believer becomes immeasurably rich in God's favour by accepting Christ, being ushered into eternal life and given the Holy Spirit.

A second possible reason was to contrast the fragility of the jars with the strength of the gospel. We are thus presented with another paradox; although jars of clay are prone to cracking, breaking, or even crumbling, God placed His immutable, unwavering purpose in them. The containers themselves (Christians) couldn't take the glory for the success of gospel.

Perhaps both opinions are possible: as weak and worthless, jars of clay are a distinct contrast from the strong and priceless gift of the gospel.

Paul reminded the Corinthians that his initial success amongst them had been based on this philosophy. The strength and pricelessness of the gospel cannot be attributed to the carrying vessel. His words serve as a reminder for us not to rely on our own strength or worldly success in order to try and sell the gospel.

APPLICATION: JARS OF CLAY

- Thank God for the jars of clay who brought the gospel to you.
- Our fragility speaks to His strength. Thank God that we can rely on His power and not our own.
- Pray for integrity like Paul's in Christian service, that our motives, message, and presentation of the gospel would be pure and simple.

We pastors are being killed by the professionalizing of the pastoral ministry. The mentality of the professional is not the mentality of the prophet. It is not the mentality of the slave of Christ. Professionalism has nothing to do with the essence and heart of Christian ministry. The more professional we long to be, the more spiritual death we will leave in our wake. For there is no professional childlikeness (Matt 18:3); there is no professional tender-heartedness (Eph 4:32); there is no professional panting after God (Ps 42:1).[6]

---

[6] John Piper, *Brothers, We Are Not Professionals* (Brentwood, TN: B&H Publishing Group, 2013), 1.

Confident

For we know that if the earthly tent we live in is destroyed, we have a building from God, an eternal house in heaven, not built by human hands. ² Meanwhile we groan, longing to be clothed instead with our heavenly dwelling, ³ because when we are clothed, we will not be found naked. ⁴ For while we are in this tent, we groan and are burdened, because we do not wish to be unclothed but to be clothed instead with our heavenly dwelling, so that what is mortal may be swallowed up by life. ⁵ Now the one who has fashioned us for this very purpose is God, who has given us the Spirit as a deposit, guaranteeing what is to come.

⁶ Therefore we are always confident and know that as long as we are at home in the body we are away from the Lord. ⁷ For we live by faith, not by sight. ⁸ We are confident, I say, and would prefer to be away from the body and at home with the Lord. ⁹ So we make it our goal to please him, whether we are at home in the body or away from it. ¹⁰ For we must all appear before the judgment seat of Christ, so that each of us may receive what is due us for the things done while in the body,

whether good or bad. [11] Since, then, we know what it is to fear the Lord, we try to persuade others. What we are is plain to God, and I hope it is also plain to your conscience.

Paul changed his tack in these verses, moving from the use of external proofs to validate his apostleship to discuss internal or personal supports. In doing so, he revealed the source of his passion for ministry.

Paul wrote of an eternal dwelling place where he longed to be, drawing on a simile which was readily apparent to him as a tentmaker. He contrasted the temporal nature of living under canvas versus living under a solid roof. He drew a comparison between our lives on the earth versus our lives in heaven.

He went on to highlight how vulnerable his current life was. He was naked and exposed and groaned for more security. He longed for an eternal house in heaven where all our shame would be covered, clothed, and left behind.

Paul drew inspiration from the prospect of an eternal life, a solid, secure, and lasting existence gifted from God and built to last.

He declared that he was confident of these things in 2 Corinthians 5:6. The Greek word translated as confident was *tharrheo*, derived from *tharsos*, which refers to boldness or being of good courage. He repeated this assertion in 2 Corinthians 5:8, reiterating his heartfelt conviction in an eternal existence.

It's worth pausing at this point in the passage and reflecting on the things in which we have confidence. We are sure that our houses will be standing when we return home from work, or our churches will be there on Sunday. We are sure there will be bills to be paid and feel confident that the grocery store will have food.

Contrast how you think about such things in comparison to your beliefs about eternity.

Paul wrote of being confident in eternal matters after he talked about God providing the gift of the Holy Spirit as a guarantee of what is to come. The order of those ideas is not coincidental. It's the Holy Spirit who provides the confidence, boldness, or firmness of purpose to hold to what is unseen.

Just as Paul was confident of an eternal life, he was also sure of judgment (2 Corinthians 5:10). The prospect of judgment brought two further motivations for Paul.

Firstly, judgment helped to keep him on track. Knowing he was accountable to God provided additional incentive for him to work as an apostle with great passion.

Secondly the prospect of others being subjected to judgment furthered Paul's motivation to see them saved.

In passing, it's worth noting that we need not fear judgment. Jesus richly blessed our future with boundless grace through His death on the cross.

Some commentators assert that the promise of 2 Corinthians 5:10 speaks to potential rewards in heaven or on the new earth. However, Paul doesn't develop this thought. If we can live confident in eternity, as Paul did, it's likely that our lives will be pleasing to our Father. This would seem to speak to a plainer life, a life lived with a clearer conscience and in contrast to one in which we were chasing rewards (2 Corinthians 5:11).

Confident: 2 Corinthians 5:1-11

We might say that Paul was trying to convince the Corinthians that there is more to faith than meets the eye. He was encouraging them to look beyond simple appearances. He hoped they might see his life not as a hypocritical performance or task-oriented mission but as a life committed to living out an eternal perspective.

He lived with a perspective that looked past temporal success and sought longer-lasting achievements—not just changed habits but changed habitations and changed lives. He lived in the reality of pending judgment, confidently believing there would be a period of reckoning when all would be asked to give an account for their lives.

In his confidence of eternity, he warns the Corinthians and ourselves not to be led astray by intellectual arguments and convincing messaging. Such earthly approaches can convince listeners of the importance of temporal pursuits at the expense of eternal ones. Instead our goal, like that of the Corinthians, is to look to Paul's example and grow in confidence of eternity and the promise of a heavenly dwelling.

APPLICATION: CONFIDENT

- Paul wrote that the Holy Spirit guarantees what's in store for us. Take your doubts to the Holy Spirit in prayer, asking for His help to grow in confidence.
- Living boldly and confidently by faith is challenging. This probably looks very different for each of us, depending on our circumstances. Ask God to show

you some small examples of how this might be possible in your life.

- To grow in confidence of eternity, we cannot depend solely on our eyes. Consider other ways in which God has communicated to you in the past and pray for the insight to hear His messaging in the future.

This is the promise that empowers us to take risks for the sake of Christ. It is not the impulse of heroism, or the lust for adventure, or the courage of self reliance, or the need to earn God's favor. It is simple trust in Christ-that in him God will do everything necessary so that we can enjoy making much of him forever. Every good poised to bless us, and every evil arrayed against us, will in the end help us boast only in the cross, magnify Christ, and glorify our Creator. Faith in these promises frees us to risk and find in our experience that it is better to lose our life than to waste it.[7]

---

[7] Piper, *Don't Waste Your Life*, 97.

Reconciliation

2 CORINTHIANS 5:12–6:2

We are not trying to commend ourselves to you again, but are giving you an opportunity to take pride in us, so that you can answer those who take pride in what is seen rather than in what is in the heart. [13] If we are "out of our mind," as some say, it is for God; if we are in our right mind, it is for you. [14] For Christ's love compels us, because we are convinced that one died for all, and therefore all died. [15] And he died for all, that those who live should no longer live for themselves but for him who died for them and was raised again.

[16] So from now on we regard no one from a worldly point of view. Though we once regarded Christ in this way, we do so no longer. [17] Therefore, if anyone is in Christ, the new creation has come: the old has gone, the new is here! [18] All this is from God, who reconciled us to himself through Christ and gave us the ministry of reconciliation: [19] that God was reconciling the world to himself in Christ, not counting people's sins against them. And he has committed to us the message of reconciliation. [20] We are therefore Christ's ambassadors, as though God were making his appeal through us. We

implore you on Christ's behalf: Be reconciled to God. [21] God made him who had no sin to be sin for us, so that in him we might become the righteousness of God.

[1] As God's co-workers we urge you not to receive God's grace in vain. [2] For he says, "In the time of my favor I heard you, and in the day of salvation I helped you." I tell you, now is the time of God's favor, now is the day of salvation.

Although Paul knew judgment was at hand, he also knew he was reconciled with the judge and had no need to fear. He was also certain he had been appointed as an ambassador to represent the judge and offer reconciliation to anyone who would listen.

Paul saw his ministry of reconciliation as being similar to the prophets of the Old Testament who were voices of God to the people of Israel. Here Paul quoted from Isaiah 49:8. In doing so, he added Isaiah to Moses and Ezekiel in his list of Old Testament messengers with whom he felt a common bond.

Similar to these great men, Paul testified to his appointment by God. He had been chosen as a specially appointed minister—not any old voice, but one selected by God and worthy therefore to be listened to and not rejected. To ignore a God-appointed messenger was surely to flirt with danger and be disrespectful of the judge.

Paul's message of reconciliation seems doubly relevant. He sought to reconcile himself with some of the Corinthians and see those Corinthians reconcile themselves with God. Although we might split these ministries, in reality they were linked; genuine reconciliation with God would bring reconciliation to the sound teaching of Paul's ministry.

Reconciliation is translated from the Greek word *kalallasso*, which comes from *kata* and *allasso*. *Allasso* refers to a change and *kata* was used as an intensifier. In secular Greek, *katallasso* was used to describe more than just an equitable settling of differences; it implied warring parties that became friends. When *katalllasso* occurred, differences of opinion were put aside and friendship was established.

Katallasso ministry isn't simply diplomacy, finding compromise in legal loopholes or imaginative language. It's not arbitration by a mediator. In reconciliation, grace must be extended in order that old grievances are let go for the purposes of the relationship.

This of course was Christ's lesson to Paul, and Christ's gift for us.

An ambassador of reconciliation is therefore an ambassador of grace. Paul's ministry speaks to his understanding of the grace bestowed on him, which in turns explains his capacity to forgive the Corinthians. It remained Paul's deepest desire to see the errant in the church reconciled to Christ. For them, he was willing to extend grace even at deep personal cost.

Paul's stellar example of a life lived in light of grace is also a reflection of the gospel we today are called to practice.

APPLICATION: RECONCILIATION

- Thank God for His ministry of reconciliation through Jesus. We are now no longer enemies but adopted in His family.
- In order to enjoy reconciliation, we will need to be selfless. This is our reflection of the grace first extended to us. Pray for a willingness to be less self-dependant and more reliant on God.
- Like grace, reconciliation requires courage. Ask God to strengthen your resolve to live more graciously. I like the idea of having the courage to lasso situations, reaching out in a spirit of reconciliation to offer grace.

To make others glad in God with an everlasting gladness, our lives must show that he is more precious than life. "Because your steadfast love is better than life, my lips will praise you" (Psalm 63:3). To do this we must make sacrificial life choices rooted in the assurance that magnifying Christ through generosity and mercy is more satisfying than selfishness. If we walk away from risk to keep ourselves safe and solvent, we will waste our lives.[8]

---

[8] Ibid., 107.

Open Wide Your Heart

2 CORINTHIANS 6:3–13

We put no stumbling block in anyone's path, so that our ministry will not be discredited. [4] Rather, as servants of God we commend ourselves in every way: in great endurance; in troubles, hardships and distresses; [5] in beatings, imprisonments and riots; in hard work, sleepless nights and hunger; [6] in purity, understanding, patience and kindness; in the Holy Spirit and in sincere love; [7] in truthful speech and in the power of God; with weapons of righteousness in the right hand and in the left; [8] through glory and dishonor, bad report and good report; genuine, yet regarded as impostors; [9] known, yet regarded as unknown; dying, and yet we live on; beaten, and yet not killed; [10] sorrowful, yet always rejoicing; poor, yet making many rich; having nothing, and yet possessing everything.

[11] We have spoken freely to you, Corinthians, and opened wide our hearts to you. [12] We are not withholding our affection from you, but you are withholding yours from us. [13] As a fair exchange—I speak as to my children—open wide your hearts also.

Paul wrote much in the preceding verses to appeal to the Corinthians and cause them to trust his teaching and not be led astray by more glamorous or worldly accounts. Paul's defence rested on the miraculous way in which he and the gospel had survived despite all who had railed against it. Paul had celebrated his fragility and marvelled at the fortitude of the cross.

He repeated a similar strategy here, with poetic elegance and crafted rhetoric. Despite trials (2 Corinthians 6:4–5), his good character had persisted in companionship with the Holy Spirit (2 Corinthians 6:6). He listed the accusations he had suffered and rebutted them with balanced virtues (2 Corinthians 6:8–10).

His insistence in 2 Corinthians 6:3 that no stumbling block would be put in the way seems to have been upheld. There is no discrediting the integrity of his ministry.

In response to his ministry, Paul asked the Corinthians to open their hearts. We might have expected him to ask the Corinthians to be open-minded. Indeed, we might have chosen that expression were we writing a similar plea today. But Paul sought not to appeal to the intellect but to the root of human devotion, the core of what makes people faithful to a cause or belief. Paul made his appeal to the emotions of the Corinthians, asking for their empathy in respect for his devotion to them and to Christ.

The Greek term for "opened wide" was the word *peplatyntai*, from *platus*, which means "broad."

In the original, 2 Corinthians 6:11 reads closer to the text found in the King James Version: *"O ye Corinthians, our mouth is open unto you, our heart is enlarged."*

Paul wrote that their message had been open, naïve, and pure, without a hidden agenda. Their retelling of the gospel was done with straightforward speech, without concealment. Their motivation was the generosity of their enlarged or *peplatyntai* hearts.

Some have translated the term enlarged hearts as "open hearts." Such was the breadth of Paul's love for the lost.

Although we read Paul making an emotional appeal to the Corinthians, we must not read this passage in isolation. Paul's appeal to the Corinthians was not that they should reciprocate Paul's love, but rather that they would be moved by God's love for them.

Paul was willing to live through the conditions he listed in 2 Corinthians 6:4–5, but not because he was working to glorify himself. He lived through his own trials because he lived to bring glory to God and seeks to see others do likewise. He didn't seek personal recognition, personal praise, or personal adulation.

His appeal for the Corinthians was for them to widen their hearts, not so they would love Paul but to love God. In accepting the Father more fully, Paul wished to see them bring glory to God.

APPLICATION: OPEN WIDE YOUR HEART

- Consider whether a goal of your Christian life is to encourage others to glorify God.
- Pray for an open mouth and big heart to enable you to minister with integrity.

•Paul set high standards for authenticity in ministry. Pray that you too would always seek to bring glory to God and not yourself, whether this be in your church or in your daily life.

Reverence

2 CORINTHIANS 6:14–7:1

Do not be yoked together with unbelievers. For what do righteousness and wickedness have in common? Or what fellowship can light have with darkness? [15] What harmony is there between Christ and Belial? Or what does a believer have in common with an unbeliever? [16] What agreement is there between the temple of God and idols? For we are the temple of the living God. As God has said: "I will live with them and walk among them, and I will be their God, and they will be my people."

[17] Therefore, "Come out from them and be separate, says the Lord. Touch no unclean thing, and I will receive you."

[18] And, "I will be a Father to you, and you will be my sons and daughters, says the Lord Almighty."

[1] Therefore, since we have these promises, dear friends, let us purify ourselves from everything that contaminates body and spirit, perfecting holiness out of reverence for God.

This passage has often been taken out of context and projected into marriage or pre-marriage scenarios. Paul's intention, though, was to distinguish between those who followed his teaching of the gospel versus those who held to a different version. By inference, those who were in Paul's camp were the believers, whereas those who held opposing views were called unbelievers.

Paul starkly contrasts the two groups, which might make us feel uncomfortable. The passage is uncompromising in its division.

Paul's version of the gospel emphasized the cross and stressed the sufficiency of Jesus. He had been at pains to explain how God, through Jesus, brokered a new covenant. This covenant was engraved on the hearts of believers through the revelation of what was achieved by the cross (Jeremiah 31:33).

Paul understood this to be a supernatural revelation given by the Holy Spirit and perpetuated by an ongoing relationship with the Spirit who Himself was a gift from God through Christ. Once revelation was given, the believer's heart yearned for God. This change of heart was reflected in an altered appearance (2 Corinthians 3:12–18) and shift to an eternal perspective (Ecclesiastes 3:11).

Paul contrasted this cross-centred, Christ-realized, Spirit-manifested revelation with his opponent's version, which appeared to emphasize worldly or secular acceptance and popularism. The value of their message appeared to be in its appeal to accepted ideals concerning money, moral freedoms, and righteous religiosity. Even moral laxity could be overlooked in Corinth if it occurred within the confines of temples which ascribed to that sort of behaviour.

Paul's self-effacing approach clashed with that of his rivals, who appeared to promote their own agendas rather than God's. They pursued worldly measures of success and condemned Paul's life as evidence of a failing philosophy, as corroboration of the faults in his teaching.

In his defence, Paul had reached a point in his arguments where he felt able to be direct with his readers. Having restated the gospel though detailing the new covenant, he drew a line to call out those who were in favour of this radical new life versus those who weren't. It was time for the Corinthians to be obedient to his teaching as God's ambassador.

Paul didn't want their allegiance out of sympathy for his cause, pity, or even respect for his accomplished rhetoric. Paul called on their obedience to reflect their new belief in a God-given, Spirit-delivered revelation. He expected their obedience as a normal reaction to the fear and awe that accompanies a revelation of God.

The Greek word translated as reverence (2 Corinthians 7:1) was *phobos*, which can also refer to fear. We might be left feeling numb by the suggestion in this verse that we should choose to obey the gospel because we fear God. But is this not the most appropriate response to a revelation of God? Our coolness toward the suggestion simply reflects how we have become unaccustomed to thinking in these terms. If we pause to consider who it is that revealed Himself in Jesus, our hearts should skip a beat—or better still, beat a little faster.

In the Old Testament, fear was the universal response to visits by angels. An interaction with the supernatural should produce uncertainty and concern. Fear was Lucy's initial response to Aslan[9] and of the hobbits to Gandalf.[10] The flames of fear can be tamed by words of reassurance, words which of themselves are only trustworthy because they are spoken by one with great power.

In the taming of fear by words, we begin to understand something of the relationship of fear and trust, which go hand in hand.

Trust is only forthcoming if we have faith that it can be upheld. Under the protection of trust, fear remains. It must remain. But the possessor of fear is no longer afraid, no longer hesitant or startled. Under trust, they are attentive, obedient, and ready to listen. Those who are under trust are ready to act out of awe and wonder, out of fear and reverence for God, who has called them.

Paul urges the Corinthians, and us, not to saddle up with those who would lead us astray. He calls on them, and us, to be obedient to the new covenant and acknowledge who it is who calls us. Our only appropriate response can be one of awe. Anything less denies the Father His worth.

APPLICATION: REVERENCE

- Take a moment to appreciate God. Draw in His majesty and reflect on His glorious creation. Give Him praise for His unfathomable grace.
- Obedience need not be the sole reflection of our reverence, but it may need to start there until godly

---

[9] C.S. Lewis, *The Lion, the Witch, and the Wardrobe* (London, UK: Diamond Books, 1996).

[10] J.R.R. Tolkien, *The Lord of the Rings* (New York, NY: Houghton Mifflin, 2004).

habits develop. Thank God for His patience with us as we develop such habits.

- Pray for a clearer understanding of the gospel in God's church. May the gospel preached by Paul be one which is recognized by all Christians.

Godly Sorrow

2 CORINTHIANS 7:2-16

Make room for us in your hearts. We have wronged no one, we have corrupted no one, we have exploited no one. ³ I do not say this to condemn you; I have said before that you have such a place in our hearts that we would live or die with you. ⁴ I have spoken to you with great frankness; I take great pride in you. I am greatly encouraged; in all our troubles my joy knows no bounds.

⁵ For when we came into Macedonia, we had no rest, but we were harassed at every turn—conflicts on the outside, fears within. ⁶ But God, who comforts the downcast, comforted us by the coming of Titus, ⁷ and not only by his coming but also by the comfort you had given him. He told us about your longing for me, your deep sorrow, your ardent concern for me, so that my joy was greater than ever.

⁸ Even if I caused you sorrow by my letter, I do not regret it. Though I did regret it—I see that my letter hurt you, but only for a little while—⁹ yet now I am happy, not because you were made sorry, but because your sorrow led you to repentance. For you became

sorrowful as God intended and so were not harmed in any way by us. [10] Godly sorrow brings repentance that leads to salvation and leaves no regret, but worldly sorrow brings death. [11] See what this godly sorrow has produced in you: what earnestness, what eagerness to clear yourselves, what indignation, what alarm, what longing, what concern, what readiness to see justice done. At every point you have proved yourselves to be innocent in this matter. [12] So even though I wrote to you, it was neither on account of the one who did the wrong nor on account of the injured party, but rather that before God you could see for yourselves how devoted to us you are. [13] By all this we are encouraged.

In addition to our own encouragement, we were especially delighted to see how happy Titus was, because his spirit has been refreshed by all of you. [14] I had boasted to him about you, and you have not embarrassed me. But just as everything we said to you was true, so our boasting about you to Titus has proved to be true as well. [15] And his affection for you is all the greater when he remembers that you were all obedient, receiving him with fear and trembling. [16] I am glad I can have complete confidence in you.

M ost days, a scenario occurs which we decide in hindsight we might have handled differently. We play out this scenario in our minds and express regret or dismay at our behaviour.

Where sinful behaviour is concerned, Paul wrote that there are two types of sorrow: worldly sorrow and godly sorrow (2 Corinthians 7:10). Worldly sorrow appears to be self-serving and temporary whereas godly sorrow produces genuine repentance and lasting purpose.

The Greek word translated as sorrow in 2 Corinthians 7:10 is *lupe*, and it implies more than simple disappointment. It could also be translated as grief, a great heaviness, or remorse. It suggests a disturbance of the soul.

Paul wasn't discussing trivial personal annoyances we might experience over a frustrating accident, or how we might feel about the loss of an ice cream scoop from the top of our cone, or the disappointment of not being able to find a favourite item of clothing before an important event. Instead he was addressing the errant behaviour in the church he had addressed in 1 Corinthians, behaviour which included the questioning of Paul's apostleship, the pursuit of licentious activities, and indifference toward other Christians.

Paul didn't spend many words explaining what he meant by worldly sorrow. He simply wrote that it wasn't compatible with salvation. Presumably this type of regret was self-oriented and sinful in and of itself. Not all sorrow is helpful or healthy as a Christian.

As Christians, so often we are called to sift our emotional responses, and this includes our response to sorrow. We are to test whether sorrowful feelings are self-seeking. Godly sorrow isn't self-serving; it primarily seeks restitution with our heavenly Father, recognizing that we have brought dishonour or distance to our relationship with Him.

Godly sorrow drives our guilty feelings when we know wrong has been done and are desperate to bring restitution. Perhaps it is godly sorrow which moves us to admit to the cashier when we have been undercharged, or what motivates us to change our movie choices or decline a second drink.

Paul explained what godly sorrow looked like in Corinthians (2 Corinthians 7:11). Rather than dismissing, denying, or diminishing their errors, the repentant Corinthians were diligent to avoid future sin. They sought to start afresh and clear themselves. They acknowledged their indiscretions with indignation toward their prior behaviour, behaviour which alarmed them and which they longed to free themselves from.

We note in Paul's description of godly sorrow that there was no self-justification, no self-pity, and no comparison with others. We observe, soberly, that godly sorrow takes responsibility for the wrongs committed and renounces them without shifting responsibility. This isn't done to seek personal honour but to resolve what was lost, to restore life and remove the regret which so readily weighs us down.

Paul painted a stark contrast between godly versus worldly sorrow. It's a perspective not commonly drawn. I wonder whether we have settled for something less in our admissions of guilt. Perhaps we have become too accustomed to accepting that any degree of sorrow is worthwhile, beneficial, or even praiseworthy. Paul would disagree.

Thankfully, some in the Corinthian church had resolved to pursue godly sorrow for their transgressions. They had been able to repent and change their behaviour to be an encouragement for Titus and, in turn, Paul. Let us hope that our own expressions of godly sorrow may be of similar encouragement to those who would pastor us.

APPLICATION: GODLY SORROW

- Consider a time when you felt sorrowful over a misdemeanour. Was your sorrow due to personal shame or could you honestly identify it as godly sorrow?
- Pray that any guilty feelings you might experience are be motivated by godly sorrow.
- It's not always helpful to play the should've/could've/would've game. Pray that when you're indulging in regret, you would have the wisdom to do so with godly sorrow and not self-pity.

Enriched

2 CORINTHIANS 8:1-15

And now, brothers and sisters, we want you to know about the grace that God has given the Macedonian churches. [2] In the midst of a very severe trial, their overflowing joy and their extreme poverty welled up in rich generosity. [3] For I testify that they gave as much as they were able, and even beyond their ability. Entirely on their own, [4] they urgently pleaded with us for the privilege of sharing in this service to the Lord's people. [5] And they exceeded our expectations: They gave themselves first of all to the Lord, and then by the will of God also to us. [6] So we urged Titus, just as he had earlier made a beginning, to bring also to completion this act of grace on your part. [7] But since you excel in everything—in faith, in speech, in knowledge, in complete earnestness and in the love we have kindled in you—see that you also excel in this grace of giving.

[8] I am not commanding you, but I want to test the sincerity of your love by comparing it with the earnestness of others. [9] For you know the grace of our Lord Jesus Christ, that though he was rich, yet for your sake

he became poor, so that you through his poverty might become rich.

[10] And here is my judgment about what is best for you in this matter. Last year you were the first not only to give but also to have the desire to do so. [11] Now finish the work, so that your eager willingness to do it may be matched by your completion of it, according to your means. [12] For if the willingness is there, the gift is acceptable according to what one has, not according to what one does not have.

[13] Our desire is not that others might be relieved while you are hard pressed, but that there might be equality. [14] At the present time your plenty will supply what they need, so that in turn their plenty will supply what you need. The goal is equality, [15] as it is written: "The one who gathered much did not have too much, and the one who gathered little did not have too little."

Paul had introduced the idea of gathering a collection for the Jerusalem church in 1 Corinthians 16:1–4. It appears he also requested a similar offering from churches in Galatia and Macedonia (Romans 15:26). The church in Jerusalem needed financial support, and the idea of the collection was both practical, to supply their material needs, and spiritual by way of acknowledging the important role the Jerusalem forefathers had played in establishing the church. The financial giving from Corinth and other Gentile churches was supposed to be an reflection of the enormous grace they had received from God through Christ.

To begin to understand the politics of this chapter, we need to step back and perceive the bigger picture to which Paul alludes in 2 Corinthians 8:8–9.

He wrote glowingly of the Macedonians in the first few verses of the chapter, not to provoke a competitive spirit but to highlight that church's genuinely enlightened hearts. It was Paul's assertion that once revelation came to the unbeliever, they would respond with generosity and love toward others in need. Furthermore, they would naturally wish to thank those who had made it possible for them to receive the gospel.

In giving generously, the Macedonians confirmed the sincerity of their commitment to Christianity. They wished to serve as a conduit of the grace they had received and make that same grace available to other communities.

In view of the Macedonian example, Paul asked whether those sincere Corinthians he addressed in 2 Corinthians 7 would respond in a similar fashion (2 Corinthians 8:8). Paul set out the example of Christ in this process, writing that Christ had abdicated His position of wealth to bring riches to those who would believe (2 Corinthians 8:9).

Far from this being a wealth-and-prosperity message, Paul was writing metaphorically of spiritual riches. Christ had abandoned His heavenly throne to become fully human so we might be convinced of the existence of God and understand something of His grace.

The second use of the word rich in 2 Corinthians 8:9 is translated from the Greek word *ploutesete*. This would be better translated as "enriched." Paul's point was to emphasize that if we wish to grow in grace, or be enriched in grace, we should give grace. In other words, we should be gracious. The role of graciousness in the proposed gift is further underlined in 2 Corinthians 8:12: *"For if the willingness is there [if grace is present], the gift is acceptable according to what one has, not according to what one does not have."*

We can also assert, using this verse, that the gift is acceptable if grace is present, no matter what one's neighbour has given.

The Macedonian gift was a breath of fresh air. It was generous and thoughtful. More importantly, it came from a pure heart. Their giving was founded on the magnitude of their gratitude for the gospel.

In this thought, I'm struck by how we are desensitized to the generosity of God's grace over time. We have forgotten how much we have enjoyed His blessings through the gospel, how we have appreciated deep joy, and how the gospel has brought a comforting peace to our hearts.

Authur John Piper would also argue that we have forgotten the grace of God's promise to continue His mighty generosity in this life and the next:

> In other words, if you want to be free from the need to stash away your money—if you want to overflow with an abundance (of grace!) for every good work (like the poor in Jerusalem)—then put your faith in future grace. Trust in the promise that "God is able to make all grace abound to you" in every moment for this very purpose.

Again don't miss the point. The key to love and generosity is not primarily looking back on bygone grace and how much God has done for you—as precious and indispensable as that is. The key is to turn from the glory and guarantee of bygone grace and put your faith firmly in future grace—that "God is able (in the future) to make all (future) grace abound to you," so that your needs are met and so that you will be able, like the amazing Macedonians, to overflow with the love of liberality. Freedom from greed comes from faith in future grace.[11]

Paul's test of sincerity to the Corinthians is also a test of our own sincerity, as well as an opportunity to revisit our attitude toward knowing the gospel. For many, the gospel ends at the cross; Christ came to live amongst us and die for our sins and we should be grateful for this gift. But the gospel doesn't stop at the cross, for Christ came so that we might know eternal life. We might experience the future grace of God both extended through our present age and into the next.

Receipt of the gospel doesn't mean that we rely on past grace to power future acts of love, for the gospel's promises extend beyond our initial salvation. They assure us of God's blessings now and in the future.

This is Paul's primary objective: to make us think again about what Christ through grace has delivered to our hearts. We are to

[11] John Piper, *Future Grace* (Colorado Springs, CO: Multnomah Books, 1995), 72.

let an acknowledgement of this drive our hearts in a gracious response.

This is how we grow in grace as Christians. We reflect the grace continually bestowed on us and faithfully live this out as grace toward others. By extending grace toward others, we become enriched with Christ's grace ourselves.

APPLICATION: ENRICHED

- Giving to the undeserving is hard. But this is grace, and opportunities to bestow it on others are probably more frequent than we would like to admit. Take a moment to thank God for the gospel and pray that we might be able to reflect some of our gratitude for it in an interaction today.
- Consider that our gratitude for the gospel is proportional to our graciousness in giving. Does this formula fairly reflect your attitude toward giving?
- Pray for a renewed sense of continued appreciation for the good news of the gospel so it might enrich your grace-filled moments toward others.

Generosity

2 CORINTHIANS 8:16–9:15

Thanks be to God, who put into the heart of Titus the same concern I have for you. [17] For Titus not only welcomed our appeal, but he is coming to you with much enthusiasm and on his own initiative. [18] And we are sending along with him the brother who is praised by all the churches for his service to the gospel. [19] What is more, he was chosen by the churches to accompany us as we carry the offering, which we administer in order to honor the Lord himself and to show our eagerness to help. [20] We want to avoid any criticism of the way we administer this liberal gift. [21] For we are taking pains to do what is right, not only in the eyes of the Lord but also in the eyes of man.

[22] In addition, we are sending with them our brother who has often proved to us in many ways that he is zealous, and now even more so because of his great confidence in you. [23] As for Titus, he is my partner and co-worker among you; as for our brothers, they are representatives of the churches and an honor to Christ. [24] Therefore show these men the proof of

your love and the reason for our pride in you, so that the churches can see it.

¹ There is no need for me to write to you about this service to the Lord's people. ² For I know your eagerness to help, and I have been boasting about it to the Macedonians, telling them that since last year you in Achaia were ready to give; and your enthusiasm has stirred most of them to action. ³ But I am sending the brothers in order that our boasting about you in this matter should not prove hollow, but that you may be ready, as I said you would be. ⁴ For if any Macedonians come with me and find you unprepared, we—not to say anything about you—would be ashamed of having been so confident. ⁵ So I thought it necessary to urge the brothers to visit you in advance and finish the arrangements for the generous gift you had promised. Then it will be ready as a generous gift, not as one grudgingly given.

⁶ Remember this: Whoever sows sparingly will also reap sparingly, and whoever sows generously will also reap generously. ⁷ Each of you should give what you have decided in your heart to give, not reluctantly or under compulsion, for God loves a cheerful giver. ⁸ And God is able to bless you abundantly, so that in all things at all times, having all that you need, you will abound in every good work. ⁹ As it is written: "They have freely scattered their gifts to the poor; their righteousness endures forever."

¹⁰ Now he who supplies seed to the sower and bread for food will also supply and increase your store of seed and will enlarge the harvest of your righteousness. ¹¹ You will be enriched in every way so that you can be generous on every occasion, and through us your generosity will result in thanksgiving to God.

¹² This service that you perform is not only supplying the needs of the Lord's people but is also overflowing in many expressions of thanks to God. ¹³ Because of the service by which you have proved yourselves, others will praise God for the obedience that accompanies your confession of the gospel of Christ, and for your generosity in sharing with them and with everyone else. ¹⁴ And in their prayers for you their hearts will go out to you, because of the surpassing grace God has given you. ¹⁵ Thanks be to God for his indescribable gift!

*H*aplotela is the Greek word translated as generosity in 2 Corinthians 9:11. Its derivative was *haplotes*, which refers to singleness. In context, it pertains to a singleness of purpose or purity of decision. Its use implies sincerity, honesty, or the lack of a hidden agenda. A gift given with *haplotela* has been donated without pretence; it is free of vanity.

This description of the heart of a pure donor reminds me of the story of the widow in Mark 12:41–45 and Luke 21:1–41. Jesus had watched the wealthy donate large amounts into the offering plate. He also saw a poor widow give a token sum. In truth, though, the woman had given generously, for she had little to give. It wasn't the monetary sum that counted but rather her pure-minded sincerity.

Paul was calling on the Corinthians to give in a similar manner. He saw financial contributions as a means of serving God (2 Corinthians 9:12). He also seemed to believe that this service took discipline, referring to it as a matter of obedience (2 Corinthians 9:13). He implied that our acts of generosity won't always flow freely in response to us feeling overwhelmed by God's gifts; we need to walk a path of obedience to ensure our compliance with this attitude toward giving.

Several challenges arise from these verses. Firstly, we should acknowledge our responsibilities to lead lives that are epitomized by giving. We are not to hoard our riches. When we give, we will need to work on the state of our hearts. Our work is not just to give more money but to give with a purity of purpose and without a hidden agenda. Seen in this light, the call to be generous in our financial giving takes on new meaning. It is the generosity of spirit which is important, not simply the monetary amount.

APPLICATION: GENEROSITY

- Purity of heart can be difficult to gauge in ourselves. Pray that God would purify your heart to enable you to make *haplotela* gifts
- Anonymizing a gift can be a way to protect against harbouring a hidden motive. Ask God to show you

other ways in which you can demonstrate integrity in your donations.

- Take stock of your financial donations. Are they a reflection of a generous, virtuous heart or a reluctant one?

Commends

By the humility and gentleness of Christ, I appeal to you—I, Paul, who am "timid" when face to face with you, but "bold" toward you when away! [2] I beg you that when I come I may not have to be as bold as I expect to be toward some people who think that we live by the standards of this world. [3] For though we live in the world, we do not wage war as the world does. [4] The weapons we fight with are not the weapons of the world. On the contrary, they have divine power to demolish strongholds. [5] We demolish arguments and every pretension that sets itself up against the knowledge of God, and we take captive every thought to make it obedient to Christ. [6] And we will be ready to punish every act of disobedience, once your obedience is complete.

[7] You are judging by appearances. If anyone is confident that they belong to Christ, they should consider again that we belong to Christ just as much as they do. [8] So even if I boast somewhat freely about the authority the Lord gave us for building you up rather than tearing you down, I will not be ashamed of it. [9] I do not want to seem to be trying to frighten you with my letters. [10]

For some say, "His letters are weighty and forceful, but in person he is unimpressive and his speaking amounts to nothing." [11] Such people should realize that what we are in our letters when we are absent, we will be in our actions when we are present.

[12] We do not dare to classify or compare ourselves with some who commend themselves. When they measure themselves by themselves and compare themselves with themselves, they are not wise. [13] We, however, will not boast beyond proper limits, but will confine our boasting to the sphere of service God himself has assigned to us, a sphere that also includes you. [14] We are not going too far in our boasting, as would be the case if we had not come to you, for we did get as far as you with the gospel of Christ. [15] Neither do we go beyond our limits by boasting of work done by others. Our hope is that, as your faith continues to grow, our sphere of activity among you will greatly expand, [16] so that we can preach the gospel in the regions beyond you. For we do not want to boast about work already done in someone else's territory. [17] But, "Let the one who boasts boast in the Lord."[18] For it is not the one who commends himself who is approved, but the one whom the Lord commends.

In 2 Corinthians 10, Paul returned to the defence of his authority and authentic nature of his evangelism. He was worried that some in the Corinthian church were using the wrong benchmarks to determine the validity of their teachers. He sensed that the solid foundations of his teachings might be undermined if the Corinthians applied worldly criteria to his outreach.

He wrote in 2 Corinthians 10:7 of the superficiality with which he was being judged. His comments carry overtones of 1 Samuel 16:7: *"The Lord does not look at the things people look at. People look at the outward appearance, but the Lord looks at the heart."*

It was possible that the superficial standards by which Paul was being judged would damage his reputation in two ways.

First, he fell short of the health-and-wealth standards of success. By these criteria, he was a failure. He was frequently persecuted, often suffered, and insisted on working for his living.

Second, his opponents accepted these criteria of worldly success.

Thus, if such standards were used as measures of God's favour, not only would Paul be seen as second-rate but his opponents would be seen as first-rate.

Paul, however, held no confidence in the belief that these superficial qualities of his opponents were authentic signs of a new covenant heart. He therefore encouraged the Corinthians to look beyond the superficial. He reminded them of the miraculous nature of his own calling. In 2 Corinthians 10:8, he pointed to a passage from Jeremiah that brought the focus back to Christ:

> "The days are coming," declares the Lord, "when I will plant the kingdoms of Israel and Judah with the offspring of people and of animals. Just as I watched over them to uproot and tear down, and to overthrow,

destroy and bring disaster, so I will watch over them to build and to plant," declares the Lord. (Jeremiah 31:27–28)

By referencing these verses, Paul indicated that he was Christ-centred and Christ-proclaiming. This pointed back to the heart of the new covenant, which we also read of in Jeremiah:

"The days are coming," declares the Lord, "when I will make a new covenant with the people of Israel and with the people of Judah. It will not be like the covenant I made with their ancestors when I took them by the hand to lead them out of Egypt, because they broke my covenant, though I was a husband to them," declares the Lord. "This is the covenant I will make with the people of Israel after that time," declares the Lord. "I will put my law in their minds and write it on their hearts. I will be their God, and they will be my people." (Jeremiah 31:31–33)

Rather than trying to put down his opponents, Paul chose to reaffirm the good news he had delivered to the Corinthians.

His gospel was to explain the promise of the new covenant and declare that Jesus had ushered in this new agreement. He used the writings of the Old Testament, like those found in Jeremiah, to demonstrate God's promises. He used his own conversion narrative and the stories he had learnt from the disciples to bring those teachings to life.

He hadn't read the gospel accounts we have today, for they weren't yet written. Paul's gospel instead focussed on the centrality of the cross and its significance as a manifestation of the new covenant.

Paul's Christianity was not a superficial story of pithy proverbs and apple pie. He was married to the idea that Christianity was primarily a change of heart, a change characterized by the transition from one's stubborn rejection of God to accepting of His lordship.

Judging by outward appearances, or boasting in outward appearances, therefore had no purpose for Paul (2 Corinthians 10:12–18). For him, the only things worth glorifying were acts of God performed by those with new hearts. To boast in oneself was out, to be replaced by satisfaction in God. Only then could a heart be truly be said to have been rewritten.

It's not wrong, per se, to be pleased or proud of an accomplished task, but one's pleasure should be found in pleasing God, not in in receiving man's praise.

> How can you believe since you accept glory from one
> another but do not seek the glory that comes from the
> only God? (John 5:44)

Paul came to this point at the end of the chapter when he spoke of an aim to be commended by the Lord (2 Corinthians 10:18).

I think this is what we hope for in our church leadership: to see signs of God's blessing in their lives. We hope to see more than superficial change in the lives of those who lead us. We hope for evidence of the new heart spoken of in Jeremiah, to be sure we are following a genuine disciple.

The Greek word translated as commends in 2 Corinthians 10:18 speaks to what authentic Christian leadership looks like. Paul used the term *sunistemi*, which is a composite word from *sun*, meaning "together," and *histemi*, which is Greek for "a place or set or stand." Thus, when God stands together with Christians, they are approved. And this isn't superficially gained by self-boasting. It's more likely to be seen with self-effacement and spiritual rebirth.

Of course we don't seek or pursue God's commendation as a reward for good works. Rather, His standing with us, His commending, is a reflection of whether we're in close relationship with Him. It follows that our distance to Him equates to the degree to which others will perceive His actions in our lives. The closer we are, the more readily God's commendation will be seen by others in how we act.

Let us be wary of using superficial or worldly ways to evaluate those who lead us and instead seek the things that Paul, and by extension God, would value. These are the small acts of grace and forgiveness which are so difficult to give unless we can access the well of a transformed heart.

APPLICATION: COMMENDS

- Pray for your pastors and teachers. Ask God to stand together with them to strengthen and bless them in their work.

- We seek for God to stand with us in our daily lives. Take some time to consider this. Certain items always accompany one another, such as knives and forks, coffee and cream, and toast and jam. So should it be for us with our Father. Pray that we would sense His commendation and appreciate this more readily.
- We make recommendations daily, whether on social media or through online reviews. As you post a review today, take a moment to reflect on your own heart, which has been rewritten and commended by Christ.

Pure and Simple

2 CORINTHIANS 11:1-33

I hope you will put up with me in a little foolishness. Yes, please put up with me! [2] I am jealous for you with a godly jealousy. I promised you to one husband, to Christ, so that I might present you as a pure virgin to him. [3] But I am afraid that just as Eve was deceived by the serpent's cunning, your minds may somehow be led astray from your sincere and pure devotion to Christ. [4] For if someone comes to you and preaches a Jesus other than the Jesus we preached, or if you receive a different spirit from the Spirit you received, or a different gospel from the one you accepted, you put up with it easily enough.

[5] I do not think I am in the least inferior to those "super-apostles." [6] I may indeed be untrained as a speaker, but I do have knowledge. We have made this perfectly clear to you in every way. [7] Was it a sin for me to lower myself in order to elevate you by preaching the gospel of God to you free of charge? [8] I robbed other churches by receiving support from them so as to serve you. [9] And when I was with you and needed something, I was not a burden to anyone, for the brothers who came

from Macedonia supplied what I needed. I have kept myself from being a burden to you in any way, and will continue to do so. [10] As surely as the truth of Christ is in me, nobody in the regions of Achaia will stop this boasting of mine. [11] Why? Because I do not love you? God knows I do!

[12] And I will keep on doing what I am doing in order to cut the ground from under those who want an opportunity to be considered equal with us in the things they boast about. [13] For such people are false apostles, deceitful workers, masquerading as apostles of Christ. [14] And no wonder, for Satan himself masquerades as an angel of light. [15] It is not surprising, then, if his servants also masquerade as servants of righteousness. Their end will be what their actions deserve.

[16] I repeat: Let no one take me for a fool. But if you do, then tolerate me just as you would a fool, so that I may do a little boasting. [17] In this self-confident boasting I am not talking as the Lord would, but as a fool. [18] Since many are boasting in the way the world does, I too will boast. [19] You gladly put up with fools since you are so wise! [20] In fact, you even put up with anyone who enslaves you or exploits you or takes advantage of you or puts on airs or slaps you in the face. [21] To my shame I admit that we were too weak for that!

Whatever anyone else dares to boast about—I am speaking as a fool—I also dare to boast about. [22] Are they Hebrews? So am I. Are they Israelites? So am I.

Are they Abraham's descendants? So am I. [23] Are they servants of Christ? (I am out of my mind to talk like this.) I am more. I have worked much harder, been in prison more frequently, been flogged more severely, and been exposed to death again and again. [24] Five times I received from the Jews the forty lashes minus one. [25] Three times I was beaten with rods, once I was pelted with stones, three times I was shipwrecked, I spent a night and a day in the open sea, [26] I have been constantly on the move. I have been in danger from rivers, in danger from bandits, in danger from my fellow Jews, in danger from Gentiles; in danger in the city, in danger in the country, in danger at sea; and in danger from false believers. [27] I have labored and toiled and have often gone without sleep; I have known hunger and thirst and have often gone without food; I have been cold and naked. [28] Besides everything else, I face daily the pressure of my concern for all the churches. [29] Who is weak, and I do not feel weak? Who is led into sin, and I do not inwardly burn?

[30] If I must boast, I will boast of the things that show my weakness. [31] The God and Father of the Lord Jesus, who is to be praised forever, knows that I am not lying. [32] In Damascus the governor under King Aretas had the city of the Damascenes guarded in order to arrest me. [33] But I was lowered in a basket from a window in the wall and slipped through his hands.

In these verses, Paul was venting his frustration. He was critical of the Corinthians for their naivety in being led astray by the physical attributes of their betrayers. He also condemned those who would seek to turn his beloved Corinthians away from their *"sincere and pure devotion to Christ"* (2 Corinthians 11:3).

The Greek word Paul used for sincere was *haplotetos,* and the one for pure was *hagnotetos.* Respectively, they may have been translated as simple and untainted to portray a faith that remains true to its origins and the core of its foundations.

Haplotetos conveys a sense of singleness, authenticity, and the absence of hypocrisy. It was also used to indicate generosity and guilelessness. We often recognize this in nature. We appreciate the simple beauty of fresh snow, for example. There is a quality to the white which is difficult to describe unless it's seen and experienced. We might also see this in the water of a clear mountain stream when we hold it up to sunlight; the sparkling water is almost crystalline as it catches the light.

Whether in the snow or in the water, we appreciate the simplicity of the beauty.

Hagnotetos communicates a state of being unadulterated and unstained. Using this same analogies of water and snow, we can appreciate that snow is untainted and the water clear. There is beauty in the absence of colours and impurities.

We can see from using the analogies of snow and water that pure and simple are related but distinctive descriptive words used to define separate but related properties. They are adjectives Paul chose in order to describe the gospel he preached.

His concern was for the Corinthians to remain colourless and clear in their perspectives of the gospel. They seemed to have become attracted by the kaleidoscope being offered by charismatic preachers. The personality traits of these teachers were taking precedence over the message of Christ.

As we reflect on these verses, we are called to revisit the pure and simple gospel and be sure to continue using it as a yardstick in our lives. Paul didn't reiterate the gospel in this passage; for more insight on this, we would have to reflect on earlier writings. But he does point out though if the Corinthians were foolish enough to base the foundations of their theology on the character of their teachers, Paul himself was more than qualified.

Paul appeared to see his weakness as the greatest witness of God's endorsement for his evangelism. In the last few verses of this chapter, he reflected on his experiences in Damascus (2 Corinthians 11:30–33), when he'd set out for the city as a persecutor to entrap the weak. He travelled in a position of power and self-importance, but he left in a different posture, humbled and weak, needing to be carried out while hidden in a basket.

He began in boldness and arrogance but left in servanthood.

This humbling experience was part of Paul's gospel message. He experienced Christ's unwarranted mercy firsthand. He was rescued, literally and spiritually. For the rest of his earthly life, Paul lived in awe of the forgiving grace of Christ's outreach on the road and His saving grace in the basket.

This was an example of the pure and simple gospel Paul was so keen for the Corinthians to grasp. The message relied on the foundation of the cross, at the foot of which we are humbled and brought to our knees. Our role, as with Paul, is not to remain gazing up at a suffering Christ but to be empowered and look outward from the cross. We look outward with the simple and pure understanding that we have the backing of Christ behind us.

This was Paul's gospel. He relied on who stood behind him and who also stood in front, who led him on and who picked him up. It was Christ's grace and not human guile.

APPLICATION: PURE AND SIMPLE

- This is the first in a series of passages addressing the qualities of Christian ministers. Pray that your minister would stick with simple and pure devotion to the gospel of Christ.
- Consider your posture before the cross. Do you feel empowered or overshadowed? There is a time for humbled confession at the foot of the cross, but there is also a time for feeling the power of the cross shine on our backs, that we might glorify Him who is behind us.
- Ask God to guard your tongue, lest you be tempted to elevate yourself over the gospel.

Do you feel most loved by God because He makes much of you or because He frees you to enjoy making much of Him forever?" This is the test of whether our craving for the love of God is a craving for the blood-bought, Spirit- wrought capacity to see and glorify God by enjoying Him forever or whether it is a craving for Him to make us the center and give us the pleasures of esteeming ourselves. Who, in the end, is the all-satisfying Treasure that we are given by the love of God: self or God?[12]

---

[12] Piper, *Brothers, We Are Not Professionals,* 15.

My Power

I must go on boasting. Although there is nothing to be gained, I will go on to visions and revelations from the Lord. [2] I know a man in Christ who fourteen years ago was caught up to the third heaven. Whether it was in the body or out of the body I do not know—God knows. [3] And I know that this man—whether in the body or apart from the body I do not know, but God knows—[4] was caught up to paradise and heard inexpressible things, things that no one is permitted to tell. [5] I will boast about a man like that, but I will not boast about myself, except about my weaknesses. [6] Even if I should choose to boast, I would not be a fool, because I would be speaking the truth. But I refrain, so no one will think more of me than is warranted by what I do or say, [7] or because of these surpassingly great revelations. Therefore, in order to keep me from becoming conceited, I was given a thorn in my flesh, a messenger of Satan, to torment me. [8] Three times I pleaded with the Lord to take it away from me. [9] But he said to me, "My grace is sufficient for you, for my power is made perfect in weakness." Therefore, I will boast all the more gladly about my weaknesses, so that Christ's power may rest on me. [10] That is why, for Christ's sake, I delight in weaknesses, in insults, in hardships, in persecutions, in difficulties. For when I am weak, then I am strong.

[11] I have made a fool of myself, but you drove me to it. I ought to have been commended by you, for I am not in the least inferior to the "super-apostles," even though I am nothing. [12] I persevered in demonstrating among you the marks of a true apostle, including signs, wonders and miracles. [13] How were you inferior to the other churches, except that I was never a burden to you? Forgive me this wrong!

Within these few verses, there are a lot of opportunities to become entangled in theological uncertainty. Paul was talking of himself being caught up into heaven. Should we therefore interpret more from his comments about the structures or levels of heavens? He also talks of having an infirmity. Was this "thorn" physical or psychological? Was it a limb deformity or something else? Was it a speech impediment or neurological condition? The possibilities seem endless, and many have been proposed and debated.

If we focus on Paul's condition or the substance of his meditation, we can easily miss the importance of 2 Corinthians 12:9: *"My grace is sufficient for you, for my power is made perfect in weakness."* In these words, I hear echoes from Psalm 121:1–2: *"I lift up my eyes to the mountains—where does my help come from? My help comes from the Lord, the Maker of heaven and earth."*

In recalling what he wrote in 2 Corinthians 12:9, Paul came to understand something of God: if he wanted to continue to grow, he would have to rely on God's grace. He was not to rely on his own fantastical spiritual experiences, marvellous though they were. He was not to rely on being high in the atmosphere (level one of heaven) or in the stars (level two) or even being in paradise with God (level three). He was to rely on God's grace.

Similarly, whatever his thorn was, whether physical or psychological or neurological, he learned that his physical performance was neither a hinderance nor a talent for God. God did not need it to express His grace through Paul to others.

Grace implies a perpetual beauty. It expresses the eternal nature of that to which it is applied. It confesses an aura of lasting perfume. In its lasting, perpetual, and universal qualities, it speaks to the divine.

You will remember that Paul faced personal attacks on his demeanour and credibility. Regarding these assaults, toward the end of his letter, he is reminded about what God told him: *"My grace is sufficient for you, for my power is made perfect in weakness."*

Paul might have also written, "My grace was, is, and will be sufficient for you. Grace is expressed in the past, present and future. It is timeless."

Paul recalled that God had promised power in grace. The Greek word used by Paul for power was *dunamis*. This was not the word for energy or authority. Rather, the word expressed stored power. From it, we derive the words dynamo and dynamite.

Reading these verses in their context challenges our application of Paul's theology. He writes that we should apply grace to others in order to grow in God's *dunamis*.

I have heard the words in this context many times and they make perfect sense. Of course I should be graceful at all times. But I have not always grasped that being gracious is a means to grow, mature, develop, and endure as a Christian. I haven't understood that grace is like a miracle food that will sustain, feed, and lift me up to do the right thing.

It seems that Paul needed to hear this from God too, so perhaps there is hope for me and you.

APPLICATION: MY POWER

- God's grace is a dynamo. Consider trying to be more gracious to see whether your walk with God becomes more inspired this week.
- God's grace is like dynamite. Consider applying grace to a conflict situation to see whether accepting, forgiving, and relenting of bitterness opens up opportunities to mine a deeper relationship in your life.
- God's grace is sufficient. Too often we look to our own resources for help. Pray for the insight to look to God for help and assistance. Consider reading all of Psalm 121.

We cannot survive as Christians if we do not find the strength to endure affliction. God's answer to this necessity on the narrow road is future grace.[13]

---

[13] Piper, *Future Grace*, 69.

Edification

Now I am ready to visit you for the third time, and I will not be a burden to you, because what I want is not your possessions but you. After all, children should not have to save up for their parents, but parents for their children. [15] So I will very gladly spend for you everything I have and expend myself as well. If I love you more, will you love me less? [16] Be that as it may, I have not been a burden to you. Yet, crafty fellow that I am, I caught you by trickery! [17] Did I exploit you through any of the men I sent to you? [18] I urged Titus to go to you and I sent our brother with him. Titus did not exploit you, did he? Did we not walk in the same footsteps by the same Spirit?

[19] Have you been thinking all along that we have been defending ourselves to you? We have been speaking in the sight of God as those in Christ; and everything we do, dear friends, is for your strengthening. [20] For I am afraid that when I come I may not find you as I want you to be, and you may not find me as you want me to be. I fear that there may be discord, jealousy, fits of rage, selfish ambition, slander, gossip, arrogance and

disorder. [21] I am afraid that when I come again my God will humble me before you, and I will be grieved over many who have sinned earlier and have not repented of the impurity, sexual sin and debauchery in which they have indulged.

[1] This will be my third visit to you. "Every matter must be established by the testimony of two or three witnesses." [2] I already gave you a warning when I was with you the second time. I now repeat it while absent: On my return I will not spare those who sinned earlier or any of the others, [3] since you are demanding proof that Christ is speaking through me. He is not weak in dealing with you, but is powerful among you. [4] For to be sure, he was crucified in weakness, yet he lives by God's power. Likewise, we are weak in him, yet by God's power we will live with him in our dealing with you.

[5] Examine yourselves to see whether you are in the faith; test yourselves. Do you not realize that Christ Jesus is in you—unless, of course, you fail the test? [6] And I trust that you will discover that we have not failed the test. [7] Now we pray to God that you will not do anything wrong—not so that people will see that we have stood the test but so that you will do what is right even though we may seem to have failed. [8] For we cannot do anything against the truth, but only for the truth. [9] We are glad whenever we are weak but you are strong; and our prayer is that you may be fully restored. [10] This is why I write these things when I am absent, that when

I come I may not have to be harsh in my use of authority—the authority the Lord gave me for building you
up, not for tearing you down.

In these closing verses, Paul reiterated his arguments by fram-
ing them one more time. He was at pains to stress that his
actions and teachings weren't for his own benefit, fame, or profit.

He used the word for "building up" twice, once in 2 Corinthians 12:19, where it's translated as "strengthening" and a
second time in 2 Corinthians 13:10. The Greek word in both
instances is the same, *oikodomes*, which some translations render
as "edification."

In English, the word edification derives from the Latin *aedi-
ficare*, meaning "to build." It is preserved in other English in words
such as edifice, which used to describe a building's ornate or period frontage.

Paul wasn't concerned with outward appearances; he was
anxious to ensure that the Corinthians had a resilient foundation
and structural moral integrity to support their faith. He was keen
to ensure that the church's footings and bones were soundly held
together.

He used another strategy in this passage to build up the
Corinthians. He provided them with a deadline to change, a
reset date, suggesting that by the time of his return they ought to
have decided whether to pursue the life he preached or continue
in an alternative direction. In doing so, he asked them to choose
whether or not they were for Christ. For those who chose not
to join with Paul's supporters, he intimated that there would be

stringent consequences, although we aren't told the exact nature of these.

This stark choice might seem at first glance to be contrary to the notion of edification. When given in a supportive environment, however, a deadline can be galvanizing. When we're presented with an ultimatum, we may feel stirred into action.

As Piper explains,

> One final word on eternal security. It is a community project. And that is why the pastoral ministry is so utterly serious and why our preaching must not be playful but earnest. We preach so that saints might persevere in faith to glory. We preach not only for their growth but because if they don't grow, they perish. If you rejoice in the sovereignty of God in salvation, then you rest in the sure word of Christ: "My sheep hear my voice, and I know them, and they follow me. I give them eternal life, and they will never perish" (John 10:27–28).[14]

Being given either a deadline or stark alternatives, such as heaven or hell, can motivate us in the correct environment to keep us moving in the heavenly direction.

We might also note that the hearing of Christ's voice, His instruction, is surely the test Paul referred to 2 Corinthians 12:5. Those who heard His voice would respond to the good Shepherd.

Although these verses comprise the beginning of Paul's signoff, they are not to be dismissed as a simple rehashing of his

---

[14] Piper, *Brothers, We Are Not Professionals,* 130.

prior points. The very salvation of the Corinthians was at risk if they didn't grow and follow Christ's voice. Given what was at stake, Paul asserted that this letter wasn't about his defence but intended for their edification (2 Corinthians 12:19). By inference, he had written 2 Corinthians for their salvation.

We might miss this in today's passage, which was written in a casual and conversational tone with multiple rhetorical questions. Paul's concern was that the Corinthians might drift from their faith given the culture of their city and the liberal views of those who had preached to them after he left the first time.

His timely reminder was for the church to be edifying, and thereby saving souls, by continuing to listen to Christ's voice.

APPLICATION: EDIFICATION

- What do you see as the purposes of the church for believers?
- How dangerous for salvation is spiritual drift? Is edification by the church a life buoy to help preserve us?
- Pray that those who preach would edify the church.

Full Restoration

2 CORINTHIANS 13:11–14

Finally, brothers and sisters, rejoice! Strive for full restoration, encourage one another, be of one mind, live in peace. And the God of love and peace will be with you.

¹² Greet one another with a holy kiss. ¹³ All God's people here send their greetings.

¹⁴ May the grace of the Lord Jesus Christ, and the love of God, and the fellowship of the Holy Spirit be with you all.

Paul wrote his letter endings with purpose. He finished 2 Corinthians in the same vein, but offering five exhortations: to rejoice, restore, encourage, unify, and live in peace.

The call for restoration catches one's attention. *Katartizesthe* is the Greek word chosen by Paul in 2 Corinthians 13:11, and it's translated as *"full restoration"* by the New International Version.

Other translations have rendered the word differently: *"be made complete"* (NASB), *"be perfect"* (KJV) or *"grow to maturity"* (NLT). It is a compound word from *kata* and *artizo*. *Kata* was used as a prefix to amplify the meaning of *artizo*. *Kata* emphasizes progress toward, or in accordance with. *Artizo* was the Greek word for restore.

Paul encouraged the Corinthians to continue to strive for complete restoration, not partial restoration or simple cosmetic fixes.

As we read in the previous chapter, Paul wanted to build up or edify the Christians in Corinth. Here he spurs them on to restore the building project.

Throughout the letter, Paul had been at pains for the Corinthains to reflect on the metaphorical house they were building as a church of God's people. He explained the firm foundations and architectural plans he had established and left with them. He rebutted the criticisms of other designers and architects (false teachers) as they'd sought to persuade the Corinthians to build in contradiction to Paul's design.

Paul didn't call for them to rebuild in accordance with his vision on the basis of his own ideas or criticisms of others. Rather, he chose to remind the Corinthians of the beauty and elegance of God's design, of which he has just the messenger. He reiterated Old Testament truths about the lifting of a veil (2 Corinthians 3:16). He recalled the promises of Isaiah (2 Corinthians 6:2). He reminded them of the new covenant (2 Corinthians 10).

Paul didn't wish to patch up the church by painting over cracks to hide the criticisms of false teachers. He hoped for the restoration to be full and complete. To do this, the church would need a renewed vision in the plans he had laid out for them, plans he had brought from God in the form of the gospel.

We might say that the Corinthian church, or some elements of it, had been experiencing some mission drift. They were off-plan and building to their hearts' content rather than by God's design.

Paul's hope in writing 2 Corinthians was to restore faith in the message he had brought, to lift the veil again so his readers might see the purposes and plans of God. Paul insisted that he was simply the draftsman to the grand designer.

He was amply qualified to sketch out the plans but was at pains to say these plans weren't his and were of a much greater design. His sufferings and persecution as a draftsman were not to dissuade the Corinthians from seeing and believing the bigger picture and the grand designer.

Full restoration happens only when we allow God in. Paul knew this and hoped the Corinthians would understand it too. He had learned the truth of its importance on the road to Damascus and carried it with him wherever he went afterward. It's a fine mission statement: "Let God in." This is what Paul tried to instill amongst the doubters in Corinth.

As a mission statement, it works well for us too. Individually or corporately, we would do well to take it to heart.

Indeed, Paul's closing line for 2 Corinthians—*"May the grace of the Lord Jesus Christ, and the love of God, and the fellowship of the Holy Spirit be with you all"* might be paraphrased as "Let God in".

APPLICATION: FULL RESTORATION

- Dwell with God for a few moments and let Him into your life so that He may bring restoration to your prayers.

Full Restoration: 2 Corinthians 13:11-14

- Reflect on Paul's strategy of not seeking to paper over cracks but aiming for full restoration of one's faith. Is there something in this for your own faith journey?
- Pray for those who minister to you in your church, that they would have time to let God in and prevent other designs veiling their view of God.

Reflections

2 CORINTHIANS

We are therefore Christ's ambassadors, as though God were making his appeal through us. We implore you on Christ's behalf: Be reconciled to God. (2 Corinthians 5:20)

As a basic principle, each volume in the *A Word from His Word* series is an attempt to prevent mission drift. These books have been conceived as a tool to help Christians reach for God's word and find reward and renewal.

Paul's letters were written with a similar premise, especially 2 Corinthians.

When I began this study, it was with some concern regarding the depth of emotion we would encounter from Paul and the possibility that we might not find much uplifting content. At the close of our readings, though, I have found deep encouragement from the lessons.

In particular, I see more clearly the challenge of avoiding mission drift. There is a richness and depth to Paul's urgent appeal to the Corinthians which we can still hear today. His message seems to carry even more poignancy as our Western society seems to want to race away from its Christian heritage.

My companion read to 2 Corinthians has been John Piper's book *Brothers, We Are Not Professionals*. While it was written for those in pastoral ministry, it contains nuggets of biblical wisdom for Christians in general. On the topic of mission drift, he writes in dramatic fashion:

> We must remember this: there is no standing still in the Christian life. Either we are advancing toward salvation, or we are drifting away to destruction. Drifting is mortal danger. "Therefore we must pay much closer attention to what we have heard, lest we drift away from it" (Hebrews 2:1). If we do not point our people to the inexhaustible riches of Christ so as to stir them up to go forward into more of God, if we do not unfold "the whole counsel of God (Acts 20:27), then we encourage drifting downstream where they will make shipwreck of their faith (1 Timothy 1:19)."[15]

Perhaps it's appropriate to be dramatic about the dangers of mission drift in our lives and those we would serve. Maybe one of the reasons mission drift occurs is that we aren't passionate enough in protecting or sticking with our mission to let God in.

In life's ups and downs, it can be challenging to continue our pursuit of maturity. This is another way of saying that we're at risk of mission drift. Having a simple mission statement for our lives can provide a staying anchor. Whether "Let God in"

---

[15] Ibid., 129.

or "Be reconciled to God," they are useful reminders to involve God in our everyday lives.

In 2 Corinthians 5:20, Paul urged the Corinthians, and us, to be reconciled to God. Our willingness to be reconciled to God shouldn't just apply to the good times, for we also need Him at our lowest points, those times when our more Corinthian traits are winning.

This letter has been a reminder to me to remain true to my life's mission and hold to the simplicity of the gospel to prevent drift. Once again, I found myself confronted by the gospel as presented by Paul to the Greeks. He was without the early gospel accounts and yet was able to expound God's promises of a new covenant in the Old Testament to explain Jesus's life, death, and resurrection.

> This is the covenant I will make with the people of Israel after that time," declares the Lord. "I will put my law in their minds and write it on their hearts. I will be their God, and they will be my people." (Jeremiah 31:33)

By accepting Jesus as saviour, we allow God to change our hearts and write His law on them. What does this mean? It means that in our decision to follow Christ, our consciences are spiritually altered by God. We incline to His ways and away from the ways of the world, beginning the process of reconciliation.

Our challenge is for our reconciliation to remain on course, so that we remain in pursuit of Him and become good ambassadors.

This is the trial that faced the Corinthian church, as well as our churches today. Remaining true to our mission isn't complicated, but it does take a conscious effort for us to be reconciled to God and not ebb with the tide.

For Further Reading

William Barclay, *The New Daily Study Bible: The Letters to the Corinthians* (Louisville, KY: Westminster John Knox Press, 2002).

Scott J. Hafemann, *2 Corinthians: NIV Application Commentary* (Grand Rapids, MI: Zondervan, 2000).

Ben Witherington III, *Conflict and Community in Corinth: A Socio-rhetorical Commentary on 1 and 2 Corinthians* (Grand Rapids, MI: William B Eerdmans, 1995).

The Greek translations in this book have been paraphrased from material found at: "Verse by Verse Commentary by Book," *Precept Austin*. Date of access: August 16, 2023 (www.preceptaustin.org/verse_by_verse).

Proceeds from the sales of this book will be donated to St. Timothy's Christian Classical Academy, Ottawa and LOCAL Church, Ottawa.

ST. TIMOTHY'S CHRISTIAN CLASSICAL ACADEMY, OTTAWA

St. Timothy's is a small interdenominational Christian school with students from Senior Kindergarten to Grade Eight. It was founded by a group of Christian families in 2005. It is a charitable organization and seeks to offer classical education in a Christian environment to children from a broad range of backgrounds. This is achieved through generous provision of tuition assistance.

The dedicated faculty at St Timothy's seeks to lead their students to revere truth, desire goodness, and rejoice in beauty. The school has been housed in several locations throughout Ottawa since its inception but would ideally seek to establish a home for itself.

In the meantime, the school continues to be a beacon for Christ in the inner city. St. Timothy's strives to bless children, parents, and the broader community so as to fulfill the ambassadorial role that Paul strove for in his pupil Timothy.

Further details can be found online: www.st-timothys.ca

LOCAL CHURCH, OTTAWA

Dr. Small and his family attend LOCAL Church, Ottawa, which was established in 2018. It is twinned with its sister campus in Tauranga Moana in New Zealand.

The church preaches and professes a Christ-focused message. It has generous ministries in local and international charitable giving. LOCAL promotes the benefits of small group discipleship ministry.

More details of the ministry and work of the church can be found online: www.localchurch.co.

A WORD FROM HIS WORD
BY GARY R. SMALL

Each chapter of *A Word from His Word* focuses on a single word or phrase from a short biblical passage. It is the author's prayer that by returning to a simplified but effective approach to Bible reading, your daily times with God's word will be invigorated. Enjoy the entire series!

NOW AVAILABLE:

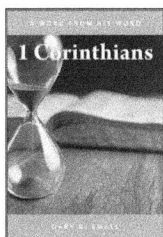

1 Corinthians	*Colossians*
Galatians	*1&2 Thessalonians*
Ephesians	*1&2 Timothy*
Philippians	*Philemon & Titus*

COMING SOON:
Romans

www.ingramcontent.com/pod-product-compliance
Lightning Source LLC
Chambersburg PA
CBHW061832040426
42447CB00012B/2929